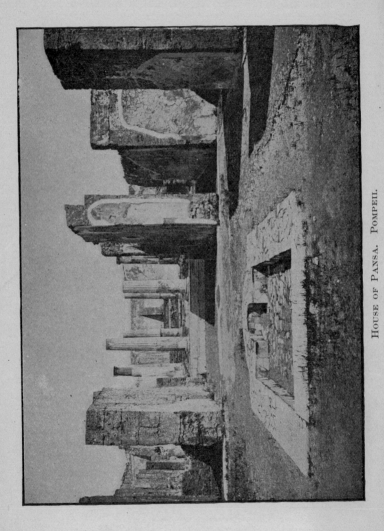

House of Pansa.  Pompeii.

The Students' Series of Latin Classics

# THE PRIVATE LIFE OF
# THE ROMANS

*WITH NUMEROUS ILLUSTRATIONS*

BY

## HARRIET WATERS PRESTON

AND

## LOUISE DODGE

οὐ πόλλ᾽ ἀλλὰ πολύ

BENJ. H. SANBORN & CO.

CHICAGO, U.S.A.

1927

COPYRIGHT, 1893,

BY LEACH, SHEWELL, & SANBORN.

Norwood Press:
J. S. Cushing & Co. — Berwick & Smith.
Boston, Mass., U.S.A.

# TABLE OF CONTENTS.

# INTRODUCTORY.

THE following brief account of the private manners and customs of the ancient Romans, their families and homes, their meat, drink, and clothing, their means of culture, amusement, etc., has been compiled, for the most part, from the latest German authorities on this interesting subject. It is especially based on the encyclopedic work of Marquardt and Mommsen, *Handbuch der Römischen Alterthümer: Siebenter Band, Privatleben der Römer*, von Joachim Marquardt. 2ᵗᵉ Auflage. Leipzig, S. Hirzel, 1886.

For illustrations of the imperial period, constant reference has also been made to the more discursive but always striking and suggestive work of Prof. Ludwig Friedländer, *Darstellungen aus der Sittengeschichte Roms, in der Zeit von August bis zum Ausgang der Antonine*. Fünfte neu bearbeitete und vermehrte Auflage. Leipzig, S. Hirzel, 1881.

The *Gallus* of Prof. W. A. Becker remains, as it has always been since its first appearance in 1838, an indispensable aid to one who would form a reasonably complete mental picture of the domestic life of classical antiquity.

Great condensation of material has, of course, been necessary; but the endeavor of the compilers has been to seize the salient points, and to furnish, within the prescribed limit of the volumes constituting this series, at least a fairly complete outline of a well-nigh inexhaustible subject.

To facilitate the student's pronunciation of the many unfamiliar Latin names of objects which have necessarily been inserted in the text, the quantity of all the long vowels has been so marked.

The illustrations have been taken chiefly from Rich's Dictionary of Classical Antiquities: a few from Baumeister, Seyffert-Nettleship, Becker, and other authors; but the source of each will generally be found indicated under the illustration itself.

An appendix has also been added containing tables of Latin weights and measures, and a Roman calendar; with approximate reductions to American measures and values, and to the modern method of computing time.

Wherever Latin authors have been directly cited by our German authorities, the references have been carefully verified. In some few cases other quotations, which appeared to ourselves peculiarly obvious and interesting, have been added; but our aim has been to insert in the present little volume just so many references to original texts as might serve to stimulate the literary curiosity of a youthful reader, yet not enough to bewilder and overpower him.

The chapter on agriculture alone has been compiled almost entirely from original sources, — Cato, Columella, Varro, and Virgil, — aided by a considerable familiarity with the rural life of modern Italy, and those farming processes of to-day, many of which differ so very little in essentials from those of Roman times.

H. W. P.
L. P. D.

LONDON, November, 1893.

# THE

# PRIVATE LIFE OF THE ROMANS.

## CHAPTER I.

### THE FAMILY.

THE first step toward making real to ourselves the life of the great Roman people must be to get a clear idea of the constitution of the family, and the relation and obligations of its members to one another. The family bond, in the eyes of a Roman of the best period, was a peculiarly strong and sacred one, and the worship of the *larēs*, or guardian spirits of the home — often conceived as the souls of departed kindred — and of the *penātēs*, or great gods, in their relation to private and family affairs, was the most vital and heartfelt part of his religion. The family was regarded as both the germ and image of the state. To furnish the state with citizens was a man's first duty. To be the last of one's line was a calamity and a curse. Family life, more especially rural family life, in the early days of the Roman commonwealth was plain and stern and pure, offering singular resemblances, in its spirit and some of its aspects, to the life upon their lonely farms of the first Puritan settlers of New England.

1

**The father of the family** was its sovereign in his own right (*suī iūris*). Wife, children, and slaves were his subjects. The legal power of the husband over the wife was expressed by the term *manus*. The bride of those primitive times was merely transferred from her father's rule to that of her husband : she ranked thenceforth as a daughter of her husband's house ; she came *in manum suam*, — "into his hand." [1] Her property became his. He might not sell, and, so long as she remained faithful, he might not slay her, but these were the only limits to his power.

The *patria potestās*, or authority of the father over his children, was even more absolute, for it included far down into historic times the legal right to sell, to repudiate, or, in the case of deformed infants and superfluous daughters, to destroy his offspring at birth. When the father lifted the new-born infant in his arms (*tollere*), it was a sign that he acknowledged and would rear and provide for it. The power of the father over his sons and their children ceased only when he himself died or lost his rights of Roman citizenship, — a forfeiture which the Italians still express by the stern phrase *morte civile*, or civil death. The father's power over his daughters ended when they married or took vestal vows. The son also might be emancipated by becoming a *flāmen*, or priest, and in certain cases with tedious and complicated ceremonies, by mutual agreement between parent and child.

---

[1] The word *manus* was at first applied exclusively to the power of the paterfamilias over the females of his own family. Afterwards it came to be used more loosely, and was often confounded with *potestās*, his power over children and slaves ; as we see from the words *ēmancipātiō* and *manūmissiō*.

Livy [1] gives an instance in the year 358 B.C., during the consulate of C. Marcius and Cn. Manlius, of a crushing fine imposed upon a father who had endeavored to evade the law forbidding a citizen to hold more than five hundred *iūgera* [2] of land, by emancipating his son and then sharing with him a thousand *iūgera*.

The authority of the master over his slaves, or *dominica potestās*, was also absolute; but it included, in theory at least, his full recognition of these as members of the family, and of his duties to them as such.

Every member of a Roman household, male or female, bond or free, appears to have had, even in the earliest times, the right to at least two names, his or her own individual appellation, and the genitive of the name of the sovereign father, husband, or master, as *Mārcus Mārcī*, Marcus son of Marcus, *Līvia Augustī*, Livia daughter of Augustus, *Mārcipor, i.e. Mārcī puer*, Marcus's *boy*, precisely in the sense in which the owner of negro slaves but lately used the same term. Later, but still early in republican times, we find the free-born Roman male possessed of three names: his own individual first name, or *praenōmen*, the name of the *gēns*, or great clan, to which he belonged, the *nōmen proprium*, or *nōmen gentīlicium*, and a *cōgnōmen*, or surname, which more narrowly defined his family, that is to say, the particular branch or division of the tribe from which he sprung; for instance, Marcus Tullius Cicero, that is Marcus of the Tullian clan, and the family of the Cicerones — originally chick-pea or vetch-growers.

**A boy-infant** received his *praenōmen* on the ninth day after birth (a girl on the eighth); the child was at the

[1] Liv. vii. 16.  [2] See table.

same time purified by lustration, which included sprink-
ling with water by means of a branch of laurel or olive,
the burning of incense, and the offering of sacrifice, a
ceremony plainly pointing to the rite of baptism.  But
the name thus given was not legally bestowed, nor publicly recorded in the archives, until the boy received the
*toga virīlis* at the age of sixteen or seventeen, and was
publicly proclaimed a citizen of the commonwealth.

The fact that the *nōmen gentīlicium*, or name of the
great patrician clan, belonged equally to the women,
freedmen, and clients of a house, led to a great restric-
tion in the first names bestowed at lustration upon its
freeborn sons.  At no period were there more than thirty
in use; these, in the time of Sulla, had dwindled to
eighteen, and even these were distributed by fixed custom among the different clans.  Thus Cæso belonged
exclusively to the Fabii and Quīnctilii, Appius, and Deci-
mus to the Claudii, Māmērcus to the Æmilii, and so on.
After plebeians were made eligible to the consulate in
367 B.C., and subsequently to all the curule magistracies,
the descendants of plebeians, who had held any curule
office formed a class called *nōbilēs* or "known men" (like
the Scottish *kent folk*).  They were thus distinguished
from the *īgnōbilēs*, those whose ancestors had never held
office, while yet they did not quite attain to the consid-
eration of the patricians, or men of high descent.   They
acquired the right, however, on which if possible they
laid more stress than the patricians themselves, of setting up in their dwellings the images of their ancestors,
beginning with the first great office-holder,[1] and, in
natural emulation of the patricians, they became quite

---

[1] This man was neither *nōbilis* nor *īgnōbilis*, but *novus homo*.

as strenuous as they in limiting the number of first names which they bestowed upon their sons in infancy. Thus the Domitii were always Gnæus or Lūcius; the Bibuli, Gāius, Lūcius, or Mārcus; and so on. The *cōgnōmen*, or surname, usually in the first instance a kind of nickname bestowed on account of some personal peculiarity, like Nāso, the long-nosed man, Torquātus, the man with a torque or necklace, came to be specially prized by the patricians as indicating in most cases an earlier origin than that of the official nobility. On the other hand, the custom came in of taking new surnames to commemorate some special warlike achievement, like Africānus or Macedonicus,— this was called *cōgnōmen ex virtūte,* — or else upon adoption, when to the three names of the adoptive father was added the gentile name of the child adopted, with the suffix *ānus.* Thus Publius Cornelius Scipio Æmilianus was the son of Lucius Æmilius Publius, adopted by Publius Cornelius Scipio.

**A daughter's name** in early Roman, as in modern times, consisted of her father's gentile name (*nōmen gentīlicium*), that is to say, of the feminine form of it, preceded by a first name of her own, — like Paula Cornelia, Paula of the Cornelian *gēns;* and so long as the old-fashioned marriage rites remained in force, by virtue of which the wife became the adopted child of her husband's house, she assumed at marriage his gentile name, as women still do in Christian countries. But this did not always, or even often, imply a change, because the ancient marriages were usually made between members of the same *gēns;* and in later times, when matrimony had become rather a civil contract than a religious rite, the wife certainly did not take her husband's name. She was known

by that of her father's *gēns*, as Calpurnia, the wife of
Cæsar, who was daughter of L. Calpurnius Piso Cæso-
ninus (a member of the *Caesōnia gēns*, adopted by L. Calpurnius Piso); or as Terentia, wife of Cicero. Even her
own individual first name was little used, until a fashion
came up, in the time of the empire, of appending it like
a *cōgnōmen* to her own gentile name, as Vespasia Polla,
Vitellia Rufilla. Sometimes, too, as a matter of family
pride, a woman used both the *nōmen* and *cōgnōmen* of
her father, like Cæcilia Metella; or one name derived
from the father and one from the mother, like Annia
Faustina. Only in late imperial times, did women of
high distinction aspire to the use of three names, as
Furia Sabina Tranquillina.

A slave, as has been said, was originally known only as
his master's "boy," — *Mārcipor, Olipor*. The elder Pliny [1]
supposes this custom to date from the time when men as
a rule had only one slave. It lasted, however, down to
the last days of the republic, and the freedman who took
his master's first and gentile name must needs append
to it the name of his own servitude, as Aulus Cæcilius
Oliper; that is, Aulus, formerly the boy of Aulus Cæcilius.
When, however, the number of slaves had multiplied
enormously, by conquest as well as by natural increase,
it became necessary to give individual names to slaves,
and these were often royal or mythological names, as
Pharnaces, Mithridates, bestowed half in derision, like
the "Cæsar" and "Pompey" of the plantation hand; or
they indicated the place from which the slave had come,
like Ephesius. Now, too, the legal term *servus* replaced
the homely and friendly *puer*, and Pharnaces, the slave of

[1] Hist. Nat. xxxiii. 26.

Publius Egnatius, was written *Pharnacēs Egnātiī Pūbliī Servus.* When a slave passed by sale or inheritance to a new owner, he or she added to the name of the latter the *cōgnōmen* of the former owner with the suffix *ānus* or *āna.* Thus Anna Liviæ Mæcenatiana was Anna, the slave of Livia, formerly owned by Mæcenas. It then became customary for the freedman to take upon his emancipation both the *nōmen* and *praenōmen* of his former master, or occasionally, in the case of a highly prized slave, the latter paid his former servant the compliment of naming him after some friend of his own. Thus Cicero when he emancipated Dionysius, the tutor of his son, called him not Marcus Tullius Dionysius, but Marcus Pomponius Dionysius, after his dearly beloved Pomponius Atticus, who was also very fond of the accomplished slave. The freedmen of a woman usually took the two names of their mistress's father, as Marcus Livius Augustæ Libertus Ismarus.

All these rules, however, remained strictly in force only so long as the family bond continued to be virtually indissoluble, and the paterfamilias was the undisputed master of his household. In the last days of the republic, with the almost unbounded facilities for divorce, the great increase in the number of freedmen, and the extension of the rights of Roman citizenship to various classes of foreigners, great irregularities in the matter of names came in, affecting alike their inheritance, their adoption, and their arrangement. The *cōgnōmina* of distinguished men were used as *praenōmina,* like Africanus Fabius Maximus, Consul in 10 B.C.; or the several sons of one father would all receive the same *praenōmen,* but would be distinguished by different *cōgnōmina,* in which case

the eldest son usually bore his father's *cōgnōmen* un-
changed, while the second son took his mother's gentile
name with the suffix *ānus*.   Thus Flavius Sabinus had
two sons by his wife Vespasia Polla.   The elder was
called Sabinus after his father, the younger Vespasianus
after his mother.   Further confusion ensued from the
increasing frequency of adoption for political and other
purposes, and from the very natural desire of the descendants of a freedman to get rid of the name which was the
badge of ancestral servitude.   *Novī hominēs*, too, liked to
assume names with historic associations, as the parvenu
of to-day orders a coat-of-arms; or to make up in the number of their appellations what these lacked in dignity,
in so much that we find persons in imperial times who
claimed as many as thirty names, one of which would
have to be selected for daily use.   Finally, the introduction of Christianity brought in names of the order of
Praise-God-Barebones, Deogratias, Quidvultdeus, which
were declined like regular Latin proper names of the
same terminations.

**A iūstum mātrimōnium,** or true marriage, could only be
made between Roman citizens (for the woman also
reckoned as a *cīvis Rōmāna*) of the legal age, not too
nearly related, and with the full approbation of the fathers
who might hold *patria potestās* over the bridal pair.   The
marriageable age was fixed by law at fourteen for the
husband and twelve for the wife, but practically it was
later, for the boy was never married before he had received the gown of manhood, and the girl but seldom
before fifteen or sixteen.   The prohibited degrees of
relationship originally included all within the sixth; that
is to say, all for which the Latin language had names, and

all which had the *iūs ōsculī*, or within which it was
allowable for men and women to kiss.

Such rigid restrictions were especially needful in those
early times, when it was so unusual for a man not to marry
in his *gēns*, or clan, that he who failed to do so was
said to *ēnūbere*, — to marry *out*, as a Quaker may marry
out of meeting. As time went on, the rules relating
to the marriage of kindred were much relaxed, and we
gather from Livy[1] that after the time of the Second
Punic war, relatives of the fourth degree, that is to
say *cōnsobrīnī*, or cousins german, might marry. When
in the year 49 A.D. the Senate sanctioned the union of
the Emperor Claudius with Agrippina, the daughter of
his brother Germanicus, marriages in the third degree
became lawful; but with these restrictions, that a woman
might marry her paternal uncle (*patruus*), but not her
maternal (*avunculus*), while a man might never marry his
aunt, whether on the father's side (*amita*), or on the
mother's (*mātertera*).

The marriage contracted under these conditions was of
two kinds : the bride either came into her husband's *manus*,
or she did not. In the first instance she passed completely out of her father's family and rule into that of
her husband; she surrendered her patrimony and became
one of her husband's legal heirs. In the second, she
remained under the rule (*in potestāte*) of her father,
and retained her own property and her right of inheritance in his estate. In the former case, according to
Cicero,[2] she became a *māterfamiliās*, in the latter she was
simply an *uxor*.

Marriage with *manus* was itself of three kinds. The

[1] Liv. xlii. 34. 2.  [2] Cic. Top. iii. 14.

most solemn and stately, and by far the most aristocratic, was the marriage by *cōnfarreātiō*, which may be compared for pomp of ceremonial to a Catholic wedding with pontifical high mass in a cathedral or collegiate church. Beside the private offerings and taking of auspices, which were seldom omitted in any sort of legal marriage, this included a public ceremony conducted by the Pontifex Maximus and the Flamen Dialis in the presence of at least ten witnesses, and it took its name from the *farreum lībum*, or cake of spelt-flour, which was carried before the newly married pair on their return from the wedding ceremony and subsequently broken and eaten between them.

There remained marriage by *ūsus*, in virtue of which the wife came into her husband's *manus* by the mutual consent of both parties, after they had lived together for a year without interruption of more than three successive days; and the marriage by *coëmptio*, which, though usually accompanied by domestic religious rites, as a modern wedding may be solemnized by a clergyman in a private house, must still be looked upon in the light of a civil contract. In this case, the father went through a form of emancipating his daughter, in favor of her future husband, after which the girl made declaration that she entered into the union of her own free will.

*Cōnfarreātiō* was the oldest as well as the most dignified and imposing of the Roman marriage rites. It was long the exclusive privilege of the patricians, and none but the children of such a marriage could ever become *flāminēs māiōrēs*, that is, priests of Jove, Mars, or Quirinus, or vestal virgins. Naturally, therefore, marriage by *cōnfarreātiō* would be the favorite form in the highest social circles.  Marriage by *ūsus*, as the simplest and least costly, would prevail, roughly speaking, among the plebeians, while the civil marriage by *coëmptio* was the one commonly practised by the intermediate classes.  But it is plain that with the loosening of the marriage tie, and the progress of what would now be called "advanced ideas," the solemn and ceremonious marriage by *cōnfarreātiō* went more and more out of fashion; so that Tacitus says [1] that in the time of Tiberius (A.D. 14–37) it had become a matter of some difficulty to find men qualified by their birth to fill the vacancies in the great priestly offices.

Marriage was regularly preceded by betrothal rites (*spōnsālia*), and children might be betrothed by their parents long before they were of marriageable age.  The engagement might be broken by either party or by the guardians of either, without involving any legal penalty, but while it lasted it imposed certain restrictions. Betrothed people might not testify against one another in the courts, and a son might not marry his father's betrothed bride.  The ceremony of betrothal was at first very simple.  The amount of the girl's dowry having been agreed upon, the boy bridegroom gave his bride a piece of money or a ring, which she wore upon her third finger.  It was only in the later imperial times that written marriage contracts were customary, and the ceremony took place in the presence of invited guests and was followed by a banquet.  There were very strong restrictions touching the days of the year when weddings might take place.  The whole month of May was forbidden and the first half of June, on account of the great

[1] Tac. Ann. iv. 16.

number of religious festivals occurring in the early summer and requiring the constant attendance of the priests. Nor could marriages be made on the *diēs parentālēs,* from the thirteenth to the twenty-first of February, when there were memorial services for deceased kindred, and offerings to their *mānēs,* nor on the three days of the year when the underworld was supposed to stand open, — namely August 24, October 5, and November 8, nor on the Kalends, Nones, or Ides of any month. Religious holidays in general were considered inappropriate for the marriage of young girls, though widows often chose them.

On the night before her bridal, the maiden laid aside her *toga praetexta,* a simple tunic, edged with purple if she were of patrician rank, and made up apparently width-wise of the cloth; her mother dressed her for the first time in a long white garment with vertical seams, called a *tunica rēcta* or *rēgilla,* and confined her flowing hair in a scarlet net. The true wedding gown, which she would assume upon the morrow, was also a white *tunica rēcta,*

Flammeum
(Rich).

gathered in at the waist by a woollen girdle which was tied in a *nōdus Herculeus,* or true-lover's knot, supposed to be a charm against the evil eye. The *flămmeum,* or wedding veil, was of thin, fine stuff and of a brilliant orange red, or flame-color, very ample, first thrown over the head from behind, and then draped gracefully about the person. The girl's hair was also dressed in a peculiar manner for her wedding. The bridegroom himself must divide it into six strands or tresses, with the point of a curved spear, called the *hasta caelibāris;* ribbons or fillets were bound between the tresses, which appear afterwards to have been braided and confined to the head. Above the braids and under the veil, the bride wore a garland of natural flowers gathered by her own hand; and the bridegroom also, at least in later times, always wore a chaplet.

The wedding ceremonies proper began in the stillness of the early morning with the taking of auspices; and this was usually done by an *haruspex*, or professional diviner, who was not a minister of the state religion. A victim was then slain for the wedding sacrifice, generally a sheep, and its skin was spread over the stools or chairs, on which the bridal pair was to sit during a portion of the religious rites to follow. The guests now assembled, the marriage contract was accepted in the presence of ten witnesses, and the bride signified her willingness to come into the *manus* of the bridegroom, and, at least theoretically, to assume his name, by repeating the very ancient formula,[1] " *Quāndō tū Gāius, ego Gāia,*" you being Gaius, I am Gaia." The right hands of the pair were then joined by a *prōnuba*, who must have been but once married; and it would seem from existing bas-reliefs, as well as from the rather obscure testimony of ancient writers, that the wedding party then adjourned to some temple or public altar, where an offering — in ancient times it was a bloodless one of spelt-cakes and fruit — was made to Jupiter; and the *flāmen diālis* offered prayers to Juno as the patron of marriage, and to Tellus and other gods of the soil. During the offering the bridal pair sat side by side; during the prayers they moved slowly around the altar accompanied by a servant

[1] Becker thinks that this formula was not pronounced until the wedded pair had entered their new home.

(*camillus*) who bore a basket (*cumera*) which contained the *ūtēnsilia* of the bride,— probably her spinning imple-

Camillus, with Acerra
(Rich).

ments and marriage gifts. A great feast, usually at her father's house, followed and lasted until nightfall. Then came the *dē-ductio*, or leading home of the bride. She was removed with a feint (sometimes, perhaps, it needed the reality) of force, from her mother's embrace, and led to her place in the nuptial procession, which was followed, first by the invited guests, and afterward, in most cases, by crowds of the common people. Torch-bearers and flute-players preceded the bride, and the whole company joined in singing *Fescennīna*, primitive and rather coarse marriage songs, probably so called from the immemorially ancient Etruscan town where they had originated. The *gamins* of the streets flocked about the bridegroom, call-ing for largess of walnuts as a sign that he himself had put away childish things; while the bride was escorted by three youths, who must be the sons of living parents (*patrimī et mātrimī*). One of these carried her rock and spindle, while the other two bore torches. The bridal torch was not, as other torches, of pine or fir, but must be made of the wood of the white thorn, which was sacred to Ceres, and a talisman against all kinds of harm. There was a contest for the possession of it, among the guests, after the wedding was over. Arrived before her new home, the bride anointed its door-posts with oil and wound them with woollen bands. She was then lifted over the threshold, a reminiscence perhaps of the rape of the Sabine women, and received from her husband in the *ātrium*, or chief living-room of the dwelling, the symbolic gifts of fire and water. According to some authorities, the two then knelt together and lighted their first hearth-fire from the white-thorn torch. It is certain that the bride said a prayer for married happiness before the symbolic bridal couch, which stood in the *ātrium*, opposite the entrance-door, and which had been previously decked by the *prōnuba*. A supper called the *repōtia* was given by the young people to their relatives on the day after their wedding, on which occasion the bride made her first offering as a matron to the household gods.

The union thus formed and sanctioned by the divine blessing was at first, and indeed for a long while, regarded as indissoluble. It assured to the Roman matron a very noble position; she was subordinate to her husband in their relations with the world, but her sway inside the home was undisputed. Her spouse, no less than her children and servants, addressed her as *domina*, or lady. No servile work was ever expected of her; but so far from being confined to one quarter of the dwelling, like the Greek women, she moved freely through it, overseeing all its activities and arrangements, the preparation of meals, the spinning of her maidens, the lessons of her children. She received her husband's guests, and sat with them at table, while the children, and sometimes even favorite slaves who had been born and reared in the house (*vernae*), were served at a sort of side-table in the same room. It was not thought seemly for a Roman matron to go out without her husband's knowledge or unattended, but upon these conditions she was free to walk abroad; place was deferentially made for her in the public ways, and the *stola mātrōnālis*, or peculiar outside garment which she wore, was supposed to be a protection from all discourtesy. She attended public games and theatrical representations; her testimony was received in the courts. She might even plead for an accused relative. If she came of a very noble race, she was entitled to a funeral sermon or public oration of eulogy after her death.

Such was the ideal wifehood of the good old Roman times; and there is a sense in which it may be said always to have remained the ideal. Everybody knows that the mother of the Gracchi and the wife of Marcus Brutus were ladies of austere fashions and immaculate minds. Nay, even as late as the fourth Christian century we find St. Jerome endeavoring to shame some of the more lawless lambs of his flock, by examples of private rectitude and dignity in the first pagan families.

But long ere that time the prevalent manners had fatally deteriorated. The institution of domestic slavery, the license consequent on the servile and civil wars, the enormous increase of wealth, and the habits of Eastern luxury which came in with the Punic and other wars of foreign conquest, all these were prolific sources of corruption; while the study of Greek philosophy, which was affected by the clever women equally with their lords, promoted the growth of novel ideas, and rendered the "daily round and common task" of the olden time particularly irksome. Marriage with *manus* and religious rites went more and more out of fashion, except for the priestly caste; marriage upon any terms was avoided by many. Divorce, on the other hand, became of daily occurrence, and could be had on the most frivolous pretexts, as the lives of the Romans whom we know most intimately, Cæsar, Pompey, and their great contemporaries, only too plainly show. Strenuous efforts were made by Augustus to restore the old standards of domestic morality, and in certain matters of personal indulgence he himself, after he was firmly seated on the imperial throne, set an honorable example of simplicity of life. He established penalties for celibacy and rewards and immunities for the fathers of three or more legitimate children; but these remedies were applied too late to arrest the inevitable progress of social decay.

Before proceeding to describe more minutely the daily habits of the Romans, and the houses in which they lived, we will add to our account of the old-fashioned marriage ceremonies a description of the rites of burial. **Nearly all we know of the funerals** of the earliest historic period is that they invariably took place by night.

Later, when there had come to be much emulation in the matter of funeral expense and display, the obsequies, at least of distinguished people, were often celebrated in the daytime, and it was reserved for the Emperor Julian to prescribe a return to the solemn custom of old, by an edict beginning with the simple words,[1] "Death is rest, and night is the time for rest."

The lighted torch always held its place in the ceremonial, as it does for the most part in Latin countries to this day, and thus it became the symbol both of wedding and of burial. Grand public funerals were the exclusive privilege of eminent men and the scions of the great families; and the funeral procession was so arranged as to afford an opportunity for the most pompous exhibition of wealth, political honors, or long descent. Even as

[1] Cod. Theod. ix. 17.5.

early as 451 B.C. there were laws inscribed on the tenth
of the Twelve Tables, limiting the sum which might be
expended on incense for burning before the bier, and
flowers to be heaped upon it, on the grave-clothes, which
were often of extraordinary splendor, on the construction
of the funeral-pile (*rogus*) in cases of cremation, on the
number of musicians, and the luxury of the funeral feast.
In the time of Sulla, further sumptuary laws were
passed to the same end.   The *aedīlēs* were required to
exercise a kind of police duty in clearing the way for the
procession, and the fire-brigade had to be in attendance
in the narrow streets of tall, wooden-roofed houses, to prevent accidents from the flaring torches, as well as to stand
guard over the ignited pyre.   All these precautions were,
however, wildly disregarded in the case of Sulla's own
costly and ostentatious funeral.

When a man of rank, whether a patrician or one of the
official nobility, had breathed his last, his eyes were closed

Conclamatio.

by the nearest of
the relatives present,
while the rest lifted
up a cry called the
*conclāmātio*, in the
forlorn hope of
awakening him
should he merely
have fallen into a trance.   The friends then retired,
and the body was left in the hands of professional
undertakers, or *libitīnāriī*, who washed, anointed, and
clothed it richly, set between the teeth — at least from
very early times — the coin to pay Charon, the ferry-
man of the Styx, and laid it on a couch of state in

the *ātrium* of the dwelling, with feet turned toward
the entrance door. Incense was kindled all about,
either in trays or on miniature altars (*acerrae*), and
flowers were used in profusion. The insignia of office
of the deceased, if he had filled public offices, were all
displayed, and also the crowns, if any, which he had won
in the public games, or which had been decreed him by
the Senate for triumphs upon the sterner field of war.
Boughs of cypress or pine were then hung up in the vestibule as a token of mourning, and the lying in state
lasted from three to eight days, during which time the
corpse was visited by kindred, clients, and friends. If
the interment or cremation were to be private, the
remains were then quickly taken away (*fūnus tacitum* or
*plēbēium*). Otherwise a herald summoned those who
were expected to join the procession by the solemn and
very ancient formula, " *Ollus Quiris lētō datus. Exse-
quiās quibus est commodum, īre iam tempus est. Ollus
ex aedibus effertur.*" "This Roman citizen is surrendered
to death. It is now time for the fitting guests to attend
his burial. He is carried forth from his house."[1]

**The order of the procession** was then arranged by a
master of ceremonies, called a *dēsīgnātor*. It closely
resembled a triumphal march. A band of music went
before with trumpets, pipes, and horns (*tubae, tībiae, et
cornua*); then came always in ancient times the hired
female mourners (*praeficae*), intoning an elegy (*naenia*) on

---

[1] *Ollus* is merely the ancient form of *ille*. *Quiris* is the obsolete
singular of *quirītēs*, the Roman in his civic capacity, or member of
one of the thirty *cūriae*. From association with this mortuary
proclamation, the word *quirītātio* came to signify a shriek or sor-
rowful cry.

the deceased; next, exactly as in a triumphal procession after a victory in the circus, came dancers and mimes, to whom a singular freedom of speech and action, even of jest, was allowed. In the fourth place, came the most significant and imposing part of the whole stately ceremony, the procession of ancestors in their *imāginēs*, or likenesses. When a man of note died, **a wax mask was immediately taken of his features,** and colored in exact resemblance to his look in life and health. This mask was affixed to a bust of wood or marble, enclosed in a marble or alabaster shrine with doors, usually shaped like a miniature house, and set up in the hall of the deceased. On the days appointed for the commemoration of the dead, these shrines were opened, and the busts crowned with flowers; and the greater the number of shrines, of course, the longer and more illustrious the line which they represented. On the occasion of a public funeral, these wax masks were removed and worn by professional actors, hired for the occasion, who might resemble the distinguished dead in stature, and would strive further to impersonate them in speech and action. The dead man seemed thus to be accompanied and ushered to his rest by a guard of honor, composed of all his famous forbears, nor was family pride always content with the images of historical personages merely, but mythical ancestors were also introduced, and Tacitus tells us [1] that Æneas and all the kings of Alba Longa figured in the funeral train of Drusus. The same great writer gives one of his most thrilling descriptions [2] of the grand funeral sixty-four years after the battle of Philippi, of the aged Junia, niece of Cato, wife of Cassius, and sister

[1] Tac. Ann. iv. 9.          [2] Tac. Ann. iii. 76.

of Marcus Brutus: "The images of twenty most illustrious families were carried before her," he says, "but Brutus and Cassius were conspicuous," — nay, his word is stronger, *praefulgēbant*, — "were illustrious, by their absence," being still under attainder on account of their complicity in the death of Cæsar.

After the ancestors, followed the memorials of the dead man's public achievements; if he were a general, the spoils he might have taken in war, and pictures of the cities he had subdued. Then came torch-bearers and lictors with lowered fasces, and, after them, the body itself, extended and exposed in rich garments upon a lofty bier, covered by a magnificent pall, and either borne by sons of the deceased or by slaves who had been set free in his will; or else it was enclosed in a coffin (*capulus*), which was surmounted by a sitting effigy of the deceased arrayed in robes of state. Last walked the mourners, all in black in early times, though white was afterwards allowed to women. The latter wore no ornaments; the men were without fasces, rings, or any insignia of office. The sons went with veiled faces; the daughters unveiled, but with streaming hair. Then came freedmen and slaves manumitted by the will of the deceased, — the latter with shaven heads, — clients, friends, the public generally, just as in a funeral of to-day. Custom imposed no check upon the expression of grief, and flowers and severed locks of hair were freely scattered upon the passing hearse or bier.

**If there were to be a public oration,** the funeral procession moved first to the forum, where the speech was delivered. Such an oration had to be authorized by a decree of the Senate, and the speaker addressed himself

to the general assembly of *Quirītēs* ("Friends, Romans,
countrymen") rather than to the relatives of the deceased. In other cases an informal eulogy was spoken
at the place of interment and addressed to the mourners
only. It is not certain that any woman of republican
times was ever honored by a formal public oration, save
those of the Julian *gēns*. The great Cæsar we know made
his *début* as an orator, at the age of eighteen, in the
eulogy of his aunt Julia, the widow of Marius. Under
the empire, however, the practice became common for the
women of the reigning family and all others of high
fashion or distinction.

From the forum the procession passed on to the place
of interment or cremation, which was, with rare excep-
tions, outside the city walls. All the great highways
leading out of Rome had come, in the last centuries of
the state, to be lined with family tombs, the vast extent and infinite splendor of some of which may still
be judged from the Castle of Sant' Angelo, which was
the mausoleum of the Emperor Hadrian, and from the
impressive ruins which border the desolate old Via
Appia. Some noblemen had private burial places of
great beauty, shady with trees, or gay with flower-beds
and fountains, enclosed upon their suburban estates; and
slaves and other dependants of the family were laid,
humbly indeed, and at a respectful distance, but within
the same precinct as their betters. The tomb was conceived as at least the temporary dwelling-place of the
dead, and often very richly furnished. The walls were
frescoed; there were lamps and candelabra, for both illu-
mination and decoration; vases of beautiful shape and
workmanship, over and above the cinerary urns, were

Tomb of Cæcilia Metella on the Via Appia.

tastefully disposed around about. The warrior had his
weapons beside him, the civic officer his badges, the
great lady her ornaments and toilet articles, the child its
toys. All these things helped to give the tomb a home-
like appearance, both on the grievous day of burial, and
on those subsequent days when religious services were
held there in memory of the dead. The remains were
either simply deposited with the couch, or *lectus,* on which
they had been
carried to the
grave, or they
were enclosed
in one of those
sculptured sar-
cophagi of
which so many
beautiful exam-
ples are still to

Sarcophagus.

be seen. The religious rites which followed, called the
*fēriae dēnicālēs,* included both a consecration of the new
resting-place and a purification of the bereaved relatives,
from their contact with death. A nine-days mourning —
the *novendial* — ensued, and was concluded by an offering
to the *mānēs,* and a funeral feast, — the *cēna novendiālis,*
— after which the mourning robes were laid aside, and
the ordinary activities of life resumed. If there were
funeral games, these too were originally celebrated on
the ninth day.

**In cases of cremation,** the simpler and probably older
fashion was to excavate a grave some three and a half
feet deep, and fill it with fuel. This was a *būstum;* the
corpse was extended on it, the fuel kindled, the bones

and ashes fell into the cavity with the coals of the dying fire, and the former were subsequently collected in an urn, which was set in the midst of the ashes. The earth was then filled in and heaped above in a *tumulus*, and the place was enclosed. These were the "vile obsequies," to use the expression of Tacitus,[1] accorded by Nero to his mother Agrippina, and the historian tells furthermore, to the shame of the Emperor, how the body was burned with indecent haste upon a dining-couch, on the very night of the murder, and how the spot remained for years unenclosed and uncared for. Cre-

Rogus.

mation upon the *rogus*, or funeral pyre, was a much more stately and costly affair. This took place upon unconsecrated ground, but near the family burial place. The *rogus* was often of elaborate and artistic con-struction, and all manner of arti-cles of luxury, spices, garments, ornaments, and rich wares of every kind, were laid thereon by friends, as last gifts to the deceased, and consumed in the general con-flagration. The coals were then quenched with water or wine, a few days' exposure to the Italian sun and air sufficed to dry the ashes, which were collected in an urn or other *cinerārium*, and deposited in the tomb before the end of the nine days' mourning.

Such were the obsequies of the rich and great. The masses laid their dead away silently, as they have done in all times, and we have already seen that *fūnus tacitum* and *fūnus plēbēium* were interchangeable terms. For the comparatively well-to-do there were those vast systems

---

[1] Tac. Ann. xiv. 9.

COLUMBARIUM.

of *columbāria*, or rows of super-imposed niches, like the
nests of a dove-cote, associated chiefly in our minds with
their hallowed usage by Christians in the catacombs, but
originally a pagan fashion, dating from early Roman
times. The *columbāria* were often constructed and
owned by joint-stock companies, who undertook to keep
them in order and sold or let the separate niches as
required. Or a great nobleman would build a *columbārium* for the reception of his slaves, by way of adjunct to
the family tomb, as may still be seen in the burying-place
of the Volusii near Perugia. For the very poor there
were simply vast common pits *(putīculī)* into which the
bodies were flung uncoffined, while the bodies of malefac-
tors, even in Horace's time,[1] were exposed unburied to
the action of the elements, and to the birds and beasts of
prey.

All through the republican period, and probably in yet
earlier times, a vast common burial place extended outside the Viminal and Esquiline gates of Rome, covering,
roughly speaking, the space now occupied by the rail-
way station and the new quarter beyond it. Mæcenas
appears to have been the first to appropriate to private
uses a portion of this ancient cemetery, which he trans-
formed into a garden or park. His example was followed
by Pallas, a freedman of Claudius, and by others, until
the whole region became a place of gardens like the
Pincian hill, and the recent dead were probably pushed
further afield.

**As between burial and cremation,** the former was the
ancient Oscan and Latian practice, and the innate preju-
dices of the Latin race appear always to have been in its

[1] Hor. Ep. i. 8, 17.

favor. In semi-Greek Etruria, on the other hand, as may be seen in great numbers of existing tombs, the two customs flourished side by side, and they did so in Rome, certainly from an early historic period. The expansion of the city and the vast increase of its population created powerful sanitary reasons in favor of cremation; but certain great families, like the Cornelii, stood out against it to the end. The underlying thought in burial seems to have been that of deep rest on the bosom of the common mother; — in burning, that of consuming the corruptible flesh in sacrifice, while the spirit ascended in vapor to the heaven out of which it came. The latter idea seems at first sight the more pious of the two; but their full belief in the resurrection of the body caused it to be rejected by the early Christians, and with the conquest of the Roman Empire by Christianity the burning of man's mortal remains went wholly out of use.

It remains to say a word concerning Roman feasts and services in commemoration, one might almost say in worship, of the dead. These were numerous and religiously observed, some public and some private. To the former belong the *parentālia*, celebrated on the *diēs parentālēs*, or days of kindred, which lasted from the thirteenth to the twenty-first of February inclusive. They began with a service of the vestal virgins at the grave of Tarpeia, and while they lasted the temples were closed, magistrates laid aside their badges of office, and weddings, as we have seen, might not take place. We seem to hear an echo of the priestly functions performed on these occasions, in the voice which weekly in every Roman Catholic church entreats the charity of common prayer for the dead "whose anniversaries occur about this time." Over

and above these public rites, there were many private
services in memory of the departed, feasts, like the
so-called *rosālēs*, occurring in the spring or early summer, when flowers are most abundant, where friends were
invited to a simple funeral banquet of bread and wine,
eggs and vegetables at the tomb of the deceased; and
roses or violets, as the case might be, were distributed to
the guests to be laid upon the grave, and offerings were
made there of water, wine, warm milk, honey, or oil.
There exists a fragment of a *cippus* or funeral stone, the
inscription upon which provides that the sleeper shall
be commemorated by sacrifices four times each year;
namely, "on the anniversary of his birthday, on rose-
day, on violet-day, and during the general *parentālia*,"
and that a lamp shall be lighted and incense burned
at his tomb on the Calends, Nones, and Ides of every
month.

## CHAPTER II.

### THE HOUSE AND EVERY-DAY LIFE.

**The ordinary Roman dwelling-house** had always been, even to the scholar, somewhat of a mystery, until the discovery of Herculaneum and Pompeii, in the middle of the eighteenth century, suddenly threw a good deal of light upon its construction and arrangements. The silent testimony of those partially ruined and long buried homes was all the more valuable because, in Pompeii, especially, they represented the average middle-class dwellings of a provincial town, commodious and even elegant as compared with the farm-houses and cottages of the rural poor, cramped and insignificant beside the costly city mansions, and the yet more extensive and extravagant mountain and seaside villas of the wealthy nobles.

The one essential feature of all these houses, the central point and distinctive mark of the Roman dwelling in all its developments, that which distinguishes it from the Greek and the houses of the farther East on the one hand, and, on the other, allies it with the houses of our own race, was the *ātrium*, long the common living-room of the entire family. The earliest Roman houses may indeed be said to have been all *ātrium*. Here, within the same four walls were assembled the family hearth and altar, the family portraits in wax and the marriage-

Street Scene in Pompeii.

bed, here the meals were cooked and served, the men lounged after labor, and the women span; the very name is probably derived from the black (*āter*) color imparted to the room, and its contents generally, by the circling smoke of the hearth fire, which had to find its way out by open door or perforated roof, since it is certain that down to comparatively modern Roman times chimney-flues were unknown.

The houses thus occupied were small and detached even in the more considerable towns. They were built of wood, or, later, of brick, mostly square in shape, and roofed with wood or thatch, carried up to a point (*culmen*) in the form of a four-sided pyramid; while a yet meaner sort, circular in shape, with conical roof and built of wattled reeds, is still represented by the miserable shelter-huts of the shepherds on the Roman Campagna. It was the typical early Roman house which Virgil conceived as the palace of Evander on the Palatine hill, in the beautiful passage,[1] where he tells how the pauper king was awakened by the light of early morning streaming through the door of his cot, and the singing of birds apon its low roof-tree. Such, too, was the so-called

Sepulchral Urn in form of Primitive House.

*Casa Rōmulea*, long preserved as a kind of sanctuary on the northwesterly slope of the Palatine. But however primitive and promiscuous the life led in these plain dwellings may appear, it was not necessarily vulgar nor

[1] Æn. viii. 455 *seq.*

lacking in a certain dignity, as those will readily understand who have entered the common room of a *podere*, or
farm, upon the Tuscan hills, or a hospitable farm-house
kitchen in Old or New England.[1]

Having thus gotten some idea of what constituted the
kernel of a Roman dwelling, let us see what the ordinary
town-house had become in the latter days of the republic.

**Its entrance-door** did not open directly from the street,
but at the end of a passage called the *ōstium* or *aditus*,
paved with tiles and flanked by rooms which were usually
let out as shops. The door was of wood, with pillars
(*postēs*) upon either side. It had regularly two leaves,
or *forēs*, which swung outward into the passage on an
arrangement of pivot and socket called a *cardō*, and were
secured, when closed, by bolts (*pessulī*) at the top and
bottom. This door led sometimes into a short continua-
tion of the passage, divided by a curtain from the *ātrium*,
and sometimes directly into the latter, now often called
the *cavaedium*, or hollow part of the dwelling, and still
constituting its main apartment.[2]

---

[1] There are scores of verses in both Horace and Virgil which
testify to the sentiment of fond reverence and unavailing regret
with which the highly civilized and sophisticated writers of the
Augustan age looked back upon the plain old-fashioned country-
life. One of the finest of these is the exquisite passage near the
end of the second Georgic, beginning with the incessantly quoted
"*O fortūnātōs nimium.*" Cicero says, however (*De Rep.* v. 2),
what was doubtless the exact truth, that the men of his time for
the most part looked back upon the old republic and its customs
as on a noble but dilapidated picture which they no longer cared
to restore.

[2] Becker and some others maintain that the *ātrium* and *cavaedium* were distinct rooms; but the latest authorities are against

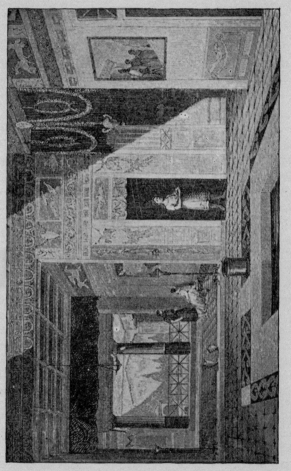

House of Tragic Poet. Pompeii.

This developed ātrium was oblong in shape, and the centre of the floor was occupied by a marble cistern (*impluvium*), with pipes under the floor for carrying off the water. Above this, in the vast majority of cases, there was no roof at all. The tiled covering of the surrounding space was supported by strong cross-beams, and sloped inward upon its four sides for convenience in conducting the rain-water into the cistern below. This, the simplest kind of roof, and the one most employed, was called a *Tūscānicum*, or Tuscan roof. Sometimes a pillar was set at each of the four corners of the *impluvium*, where the beams intersected, in which case the *ātrium* was said to be *tetrāstȳlon*, or four-columned. Sometimes the beams were not extended to the wall, but merely supported by a row of pillars around the *impluvium*. This was a Corinthian *ātrium*. In other cases the *ātrium* was *displuviātum ;* that is, the roof sloped outward, and the rain-water ran into gutters under the eaves and was carried off by pipes, as in a modern house; the whole system of roof and pipes being called, in any case, the *compluvium*. The last kind of roof alone was occasionally carried up to a point above the central basin, and the *ātrium*, thus completely roofed in, was called *tēstūdineātum*. How the *ātrium* was lighted in this case we do not exactly know. It is probable that the small flanking chambers, presently to be described, had no

them. Doubtless there were spacious houses with two halls, that is to say, with a sort of ante-chamber between the *ōstium* and *cavaedium*. Pliny's Laurentian villa we know was arranged in this way, but the progress of Pompeian excavation seems to have rendered it certain that the average Roman town-house had no such luxury.

second-story rooms above them, and that there may have
been a row of windows or apertures under the roof, like
the clere-story windows of a cathedral.   In the far more
numerous cases where the *ātrium* was lighted simply by
the opening above the *impluvium*, there were always
arrangements, as in the theatres, for drawing an awning,
or *vēlum*, across the open space, as a protection from the
sun.   The *ātrium* in one or other of these forms was
still the place where guests were received, where certain
rites of domestic worship were celebrated, and where
the dead lay in state.   But the cooking was now done in
a kitchen (*culīna*) at the back of the establishment, and
the hearth-stone, where sacrifices to the household gods
had been made in primitive times, was represented by
a marble altar, set against the rear wall of the apartment

On either side of the *ātrium*, down about two-thirds of
its length, ran a row of small square rooms, the sitting,
sleeping, and guest rooms of the establishment.   These
opened into the hall either by doors or portières, and
from one of them ascended the steep and narrow stairs,
which led to the upper story.   Beyond this range of
diminutive rooms, on either side, the *ātrium* broadened
out into two *ālae*, wings or alcoves, in the comparative
seclusion of which were now arranged the portrait busts
of the ancestors in their several niches or shrines, and so
ordered, in cases of long descent, as to present the semblance of a family tree; while bronze tablets, recording
the names and deeds of the persons commemorated, were
set in the wall beneath their respective shrines.

**Between the two ālae, directly opposite the entrance-
door, was the opening into the tablīnum,** which was
usually divided from the *ātrium* by curtains only.   In

old-fashioned country houses of the better sort, the *tablī-num* had been represented by a sort of open porch or veranda, often a simple *pergula*, roofed by a trellis for vines, which ran all along the back of the modest dwelling, and led to the gardens or orchards behind it. Under the roof of this porch the rustic "Squire," to whom, as always happens, it fell naturally to enact the magistrate, heard complaints and decided differences between his tenants and humble neighbors; and the *tabulae*, or records of his decisions, were deposited there. Later, when the dwelling had considerably developed, and the simple back porch had become only one side of a quadrangular colonnade, surrounding an open court, the *tabulae* were removed to the interior of the dwelling, and the room where they were kept took its name from them, *tablīnum*. In this, and the corresponding room of a town-house, other family archives came also to be deposited, and here were put upon record those curious contracts for mutual hospitality — *hospitia prīvāta*, — which will be described in another chapter. Here, too, stood the strong-box of the master of the mansion, and the *tablīnum* was in some sort his study or den. It could be shut off from all the rest of the house, from the *ātrium* by the heavy curtain or curtains already mentioned, from the open court at the back by folding doors; and it was flanked by two narrow passages (*faucēs*) with doors at either end, through which the family and the domestic slaves could pass and re-pass between the *ātrium* and the rear portion of the house. But if the curtains in front of the *tablīnum* were withdrawn, and the doors at the back thrown open, he who entered the house from the front had an uninterrupted, and, what must have

been on a bright day, a very charming view across the
*ātrium*, filled with the diffused and softly colored light
which filtered through the *vēlum* overhead, and down the
vista of the *tablīnum*, to the fountain, flowers, and shrub-
bery, which occupied the centre of the great pillared court,
or *peristȳlum*, beyond.

**The peristyle** had now become quite as important a
member of the dwelling as the *ātrium*. Whoever has
seen the garden-court of an Italian villa or palace,[1] or a
green convent or college cloister, and has also seen Pompeii, will have an approximate idea of the general aspect
of a peristyle.

The ambulatory, or surrounding promenade, was much
narrower than the covered part of the *ātrium*, the open
space, of course, proportionally larger. From the peristyle, and usually on its right, opened the *triclīnium*, or
principal dining-room of the house, the neighboring
kitchen, or *culīna*, and the *sacrārium*, or chapel, where
the images of the gods were set up, and sacrifices and
other ceremonies of private worship were actually performed; for the altar in the *ātrium* seems rather to have
been a reminiscence of the hearth, and an ornamental
symbol of devotion, than intended for frequent use.

From under the colonnade on the opposite, or left-
hand, side opened storerooms of various kinds and a
second stair which sometimes led to inferior sleeping-
rooms upon the upper story. At the back of the peristyle there was usually an open garden.

Such being the typical arrangement of the Roman
dwelling, there was room, as in our modern houses, for
great variations of detail, and it is easy to understand

---

[1] The beautiful court of the post-office at Rome is a good example.

the sort of change which would be introduced by the
increase of wealth, the adoption of Eastern fashions, and
the enormous growth of private luxury. **To begin with
the entrance :** — the shallow, sunken porch before the
*ōstium,* formed by the projection of the shops on either
side, would now be expanded into a spacious vestibule
with marble floor, richly adorned with statues and por-
trait-busts, prizes of prowess and trophies of arms, even
the state chariot which had borne the master of the house
on occasions of public triumph sometimes found a place
here; and it was here that the countless throng of friends,
clients, and other *protégés* and dependants who hung
upon the footsteps of a distinguished citizen in later days,
waited, sometimes from before daylight, to give the *salūtātiō,* or morning greeting, to the great man when he came
out. The plain door-posts were now sheathed with rich
carvings (*antepagmenta*), or adorned with intricate and
costly inlaid work.[1] There were no shops, of course,
attached to houses of such grandeur; but the rooms on
either side of the entrance became, the one a lodge for the
*ōstiārius,* or porter, while the other was often used by
the master of the mansion as a species of office, where
he received and examined the accounts presented by the
stewards of his various rural properties, and took the
money for his valuable crops. The town-palace of an
Italian nobleman has, to this day, a similar room upon
its ground-floor used for almost precisely the same
purposes.

The stately dwelling we are now considering had an
indefinitely increased number of living, withdrawing, and
guest rooms, opening off the *cavaedium* and peristyle.

[1] See Verg. G. ii. 463.

There were bedrooms for rest both by day and by night (*cubicula diurna* and *cubicula nocturna*) and dining-rooms with different exposures for summer and winter, and with dimensions to suit the various numbers of guests which might be entertained. There were often (we find instances even in provincial Pompeii) two peristyles, in which case the anterior usually gave access to a picture-gallery (*pinacothēca*) and a library (*bibliothēca*), the names betraying that the fashion was adopted from Greece.

**The earliest private** *bibliothēcae* were small and plain, seemingly intended as mere depositories of books, and not at all as luxurious retreats for study or literary recreation. The walls were lined with low cupboards (*armāria*) or cases of open shelves, for the reception of papyrus rolls; and sometimes a double row of such receptacles occupied the centre of the room. Not much before Cicero's time did men begin to vie with one another in the elegance of their library appointments, and to adorn the room with pictures and statues.

**The substance on which the books of this time were written** was almost invariably the fine bark (*liber*) of the Egyptian papyrus, of which the long fibres were first woven together basket-wise, and then spread upon some flat surface and pressed into the proper consistency. The sheet thus obtained was dried in the sun, smoothed, and cut into strips (*pāginae*), which were written upon one side only, glued together at the ends and tightly rolled over a hollow reed. The width of the strips varied from six to thirteen inches, and if a yet broader page were required it was made by gluing these together lengthwise, after they were written. The text was thus presented in parallel columns which were usually divided by scarlet lines. Through the hollow of the reed ran a rod (*umbilīcus*), which furnished the axis on which the book turned in rolling or unrolling. The projecting ends of this rod were called the *cornua*, and they were often painted or gilded, or furnished with metal or ivory nuts. The ends of the papyrus roll itself were carefully evened and dyed black; and the outer covering was of parchment, which was colored in some brilliant hue, usually purple or yellow, while the title of the book was written in scarlet ink upon a small separate slip of parchment and attached to one of the *cornua*.

We hear of instances in which an entire work, like the Iliad or the History of Thucydides, was copied upon a single roll, that of the historian being more than eighty-eight yards long. But such a book would, of course, be too unwieldy for ordinary use, and the common way was to divide the works of a prolific writer into several rolls, or *volūmina*, which were all kept for convenience in one light cylindrical wooden box, a *capsa* or *scrīnium*, somewhat resembling a modern band-box. The ink (*ātrāmentum librārium*) was rather thick, and made, like

Writing Materials.

the ink of the Chinese, of lamp-black or sepia; the pens were slender reeds, or *calamī*, cut and pointed like a goose-quill. After parchment came into general use, the custom of rolling was for the most part abandoned, and the *pāginae* were simply fastened together at the back like a modern book. Such an arrangement was and is called a *cōdex*.

**The domestic slaves** were lodged in tiny cells around the posterior peristyle, rather than on the upper floor, where the regular sleeping-rooms of the family seem usually to have been. There would be extensive and beautiful grounds at the rear of such a mansion, laid out in the perpetual Italian taste, embellished with trellises, fountains, and statues, and often overshadowed by magnificent trees, like the six ancient and enormous lotus trees in the town-gardens of the orator Crassus upon the Palatine, which were valued at three million sesterces, or about $20,000 apiece, and which lived and flourished until they were consumed by Nero's fire in 64 A.D.

In Rome and the larger towns, however, as in modern cities, especially those of the continent of Europe, the detached dwellings came to be far outnumbered by the *insulae*, or apartment-houses, which were often several stories high, with shops upon the street level, and lodgings of various grades behind and above. The crowded tenements of the very poor were to be found in the meaner of these *insulae*, while there were others in the more expensive wards (*regiōnēs*) where young men of fashion, like Cicero's friend Cælius, had commodious apartments, which probably corresponded very fairly with the bachelor quarters occupied by men of the same class to-day.

In trying to represent to ourselves more exactly the interior aspect of a completely appointed Roman house, we have first to remember the rich effect of its marble-wainscoted and frescoed walls; the broad panels of pure deep color, usually yellow or red, with graceful central figures, and surrounded by brilliant and delicate arabesques, which we find almost universal in Pompeii,

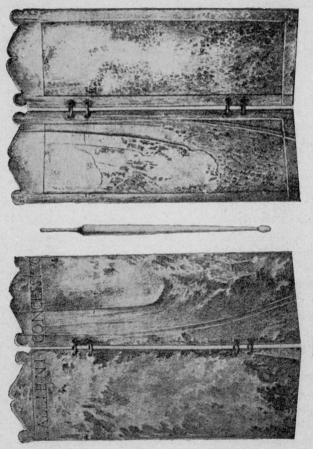

WRITING TABLETS, SHOWING INSIDE AND OUTSIDE.

even in houses of modest pretensions. There was color also and grace of design in the various kinds of mosaic floors, of which so many specimens are still to be seen, and though the furnishing of the rooms may seem simple and even scanty to our jumbled modern ideas, the separate pieces were for the most part so excellent in design and so beautiful in workmanship that they well deserved to be set wide apart and relieved, each one, against an artistic background.

**The articles of furniture** in common use may be comprised under a very few heads : *lectī*, beds and couches ; *sedīlia*, or seats ; *mēnsae*, tables ; *arcae* and *armāriī*, chests and cabinets ; *lucernae*, lamps, whether standing or depending.

Couches included the *lectī triclīniārēs*, or low dining-couches covered with tapestry and heaped with cushions, on which both men and women reclined at formal meals ; the *lectī cubiculārēs*, true beds of rest, for slumber at night or siesta by day ; and the *lectulī* or *lectī lūcubrātōriī*, which had commonly two arms and no back, and were used chiefly for reading or writing at night, when the student reclined his back against one of the arms and supported his tablet or manuscript upon one uplifted knee. And since it was thus that inveterate letter-writers like Cicero and the younger Pliny carried on most of their correspondence, this may be as good a place as any other in which to describe the form of the Roman letter.

**The tablets** in question were light, rectangular boards with slightly elevated frames, like a modern slate, and they were spread with a thin coating of wax, on which written characters were traced with a *stilus*, or pointed stick of wood or ivory. One such tablet would serve for the jotting down of hurried notes, or for a schoolboy's exercise. A lengthy letter was composed of several, united at the back, like the leaves of a *cōdex* or a modern book, by means of straps or strings passed through holes in the frame. The inner tablets might be waxed and written upon both sides; the outer, upon the inside only. They were bound together by a strong cord, which for greater security was passed through one or more holes bored in the tablet itself; the ends of the cord were fastened down with wax, which was imprinted with the writer's seal, and the message was conveyed to its destination by a *tabellārius,* or letter-carrier. In later times these rather unwieldy tablets were superseded by sheets of papyrus.

**The frames of the various kinds of couches** were regularly made of wood, often carved or inlaid with

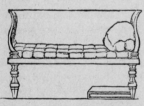

Lectus Cubicularis.

ivory or brass, and supported sometimes upon ivory feet. The frames were strung with girths or bands (*fasciae, lōra*), on which were laid a mattress (*torus*) and a bolster (*cervīcal*) and *vestēs strāgulae,* or coverings, of more or less magnificence. Beds for slumber, though tolerably broad, were open for the most part upon one side only, being provided with a tall back and arms, like an old-fashioned sofa; and they stood higher upon their carved or elaborately turned legs than even the four-posters of our own ancestors, insomuch that they could only be scaled by

help of a footstool, or even a step-ladder. Bedsteads
of bronze and even of the precious metals were used
in later times; and seats and chairs were made of all
these different materials and often decorated with great
luxury, while in form they ranged from the simple *sub-
sellium*, or four-legged stool, to the *cathedra*, or deep,
commodious chair, like that in which the elder Agrippina may be seen sitting with so much grace and dignity
in the museum of the Capitol at Rome, or Livia, the
exquisitely beautiful, in the seclusion of the Torlonia
gallery.

**Under the general head of tables** were included the
*abacus*, or side-board, in shape somewhat like a pier or
console table, the *mēnsa delphica*, or three-legged table,
and the *monopodium*, supported on a single standard in
the centre. Tables of the latter shape were often small,
extremely precious in material, and elegant in design;
and one such formed part of the furniture of every
decent bedroom, and supported, from the time when
candles of tallow or wax went somewhat out of fashion,
one of the boat-shaped oil lamps of pottery or bronze,
with gracefully turned handle (*ānsa*) at one end, and
at the other an opening (*rōstrum, nāsus*) for the wick
(*ellychnium*), which abound in Pompeii and in existing
tombs. A *candēlābrum* was a tall slender stand of wood
or metal, usually provided with three claw feet which
rested on the floor. In shape and size it corresponded
with the standard of a piano-lamp of the present day,
which, indeed, is often exactly copied from it. The
*candēlābrum* carried atop either a small tray for sup-
porting such a lamp as has been already described, or
a spike for a large wax candle, like an altar candlestick.

A shorter kind of *candēlābrum*, often very elaborately wrought, stood upon a chest or sideboard, and had two or more branches from which small hanging lamps were suspended.

Bronze Lamp.

The chest and the cabinet offered, as they have always done, a favorable field for the most elaborate and costly decoration; and these massive articles doubtless possessed in a handsome Roman house exactly the importance which they still retain in grand Italian interiors.

**The table-ware** of the affluent had become, in the last days of the republic, extraordinarily luxurious. Something more will be said upon this head in the chapter on food. Here it may suffice to remark that, to judge by the revelations of Pompeii, almost every household implement in daily use at the time of the catastrophe had an artistic significance due to the beauty of its design, over and above its practical value. But the fashion of these articles was to some extent exotic. Their shapes were borrowed from the booty taken in foreign conquest, or else they were the handiwork of

Greek captives, or of artisans who had learned their methods from them.

**In primitive Roman times the day was divided** in the simplest manner, so as to meet the needs and facilitate the labors of the tiller of the soil. The husbandman rose at sunrise, worked a certain number of hours before his morning meal, returned to the field after this, and worked until noontide, when he ate again and slept awhile, arising refreshed for another period of labor in the cool of the afternoon, which lasted until sunset and supper-time. Relief to the monotony of this daily round came in the shape of numerous holidays, both public and private. To the former class belonged the general celebrations, bearing more or less of a religious character, like the *Compitālia* in January, the *Mātrōnālia* in March, the *Vīnālia Rūstica* in August, and the *Sāturnālia* in December; to the latter, all the birthday, betrothal, wedding, house-warming, and New Year's gatherings, with their appropriate suppers and sacrifices, and exchange of gifts and congratulations, as well as the reception given when a youth assumed the garb of manhood, and the banquets already noted in commemoration of the dead.

But with the rise of great towns, the growth of commerce and manufactures, the introduction of new industries, and of new diversions also, and the ever-increasing complexity and expense of existence, the old bucolic arrangement of the day passed wholly out of date, especially among the so-called privileged classes, insomuch that in the time of Nero we find a would-be philosopher like Seneca complaining[1] that, whereas human occupa-

[1] Sen. Ep. cxxii. 10.

tions used to be regulated by natural laws, now the object appeared to be to make one's habits as artificial as possible. Daybreak, he says, is bedtime. As evening approaches we begin to show signs of activity. Toward morning we dine. "*Nōn oportet id facere quod populus*," "Come what may, we mustn't do as the common people do."

Up to the time when the first sun-dial appeared in Rome, 263 B.C., there was no division of the day into hours; and even after this the Romans continued to make a distinction between the natural and the civil day. The former was reckoned from midnight to midnight — twenty-four hours; the latter from sunrise to sunset — twelve hours. Practically, the period of daylight still fell into the four natural divisions established by the necessities of rural life, of morning, forenoon, afternoon, and evening; while the four military watches (*vigiliae*) measured the night. But in the course of the ensuing century, sun-dials (*sōlāria*) and hour-glasses (*clepsydrae*), whether for sand or water, came into general use; and some sort of time-keeper, or *hōrologium* — a name which comprised both dials and hour-glasses — was to be found, not merely upon all public squares and buildings, but in every private house. There was this great difference, however, between the Roman measurement of time and our own — an hour was not a fixed period of unvarying length. It was always considered as the twelfth part of the time from sunrise to sunset, and again of that from sunset to sunrise. The hours of a winter day were therefore actually short, while those of a summer day were long; the converse, of course, being true of the nights. At the equinoxes, when the days and nights

were of the same length, a Roman hour contained sixty
of our minutes. At the summer solstice the hours of
the day contained seventy-five and a half, and at the
winter solstice forty-four and a half minutes. In the
former case day began at 4.27 A.M., according to our
reckoning, and ended at 7.33 P.M.; in the latter it began
at 7.33 and ended at 4.27. This peculiarity must always
be borne in mind, when one would fix in the memory the
hour at which a given event occurred.

Seneca's lament to the contrary notwithstanding, **the
Romans were for the most part early risers.** Only the
idle and the very luxurious, or those who had to sleep
off the debauch of the previous night, were wont to lie in
bed even until broad daylight. Artisans and shop-keepers
went to their work by candle-light. Men of letters, like
Cicero, Horace, the elder Pliny, the Emperor Marcus
Aurelius, preferred to all others the hours before sunrise for reading and writing. The schools began at a
very early hour,[1] so did theatrical representations (*prīmā
lūce*), and all the family festivals already noted; and in
Christian times the daily morning service in the churches.
The courts of justice sat from the third to the tenth hour;
that is, roughly, from seven to five in summer and nine
to four in winter. On the days of general election, the
*comitia* began, or, as we should say, the polls opened at
sunrise, and did not close till dusk. The sessions of the
Senate also began early and continued till sunset.

In primitive times the master of the house expected
to receive good-morrow from his children and servants

---

[1] "Up," says Martial, in the last epigram of his fourteenth book;
"for the baker is selling the schoolboys their breakfast, and chan-
ticleer proclaims the dawn."

at daybreak, after which he offered the morning sacrifice, and then assigned to his various people their duties for the day. A reminiscence of this custom appears always to have survived in certain of the old families, and it was adopted in the strictly ordered households of the Antonine Cæsars. Out of it grew the ceremonious *salūtātiō* of late republican and early imperial times, the self-interested compliments of the morning offered to an influential citizen by the clients and other lesser folk, who thronged his hall and competed for his favor; and the earlier the *salūtātiō* could be made, the better. We read therefore of the Roman streets being alive before light in winter with the hurrying figures of carefully attired clients, who elbowed one another in the stately vestibule of their patron, until the doors were flung open into the *ātrium*, where he stood to receive them. They then defiled before him, each making his bow and uttering his *avē*, *domine*, to which the magnate responded by a hand-shake and a word of courtesy — sometimes by a kiss. He made a point of addressing each man by name, and if he hesitated for one instant, he was prompted by the *nōmenclātor* at his ear, a slave whose business it was to know the proper appellation of every person present.

Before going through with this wearisome performance the patron had probably taken his *iēntāculum*, or first breakfast, in the privacy of his own chamber. The client would have to snatch his where he could in passing from one house to another, — for many paid their daily court to more than one great man, — often doubtless in the bakeries or cake-shops patronized by the schoolboys. **This first meal of the day** was invariably, as it still is in Latin countries, a very simple one. It consisted of bread with salt, or dipped in wine, olives or dates, possibly honey, and a bit of cheese. Hearty food, such as warm and cold meats, fish, vegetables, fresh fruit, and wine, was rarely taken much before mid-day. In early times, and always among the farming population, this mid-day meal constituted the *cēna*, the dinner, or principal meal of the day, while a supper, or *vesperna*, was served in the evening after work was done. The exigencies of city life caused the noon *cēna* to be replaced by the *prandium*, lunch or second breakfast, consisting indeed of much the same sort of viands, while the dinner, or *cēna* proper, became vastly more elaborate, and was deferred until toward evening.

Three meals a day were perhaps the rule among the well-to-do, yet physicians often counselled only two, except for the old and weak, and many city-folk — even the comparatively affluent — confined themselves to a *prandium*, taken about eleven o'clock, and a late *cēna*. The natural Roman appears to have been, like the average Italian of to-day, an abstemious creature. Only the wanton and extravagant *gourmands* of the decadence dreamed of adding to the interminable courses and fantastic luxury of their *cēna* a late supper, or *cōmissātiō*, served often in the " wee sma' hours ayant the twal'."

After the *prandium*, the world retired for its *merīdiātiō*, or **mid-day slumber**. This custom was well-nigh a universal one. It belonged both to city and to country life, and dated from the earliest historic period. Only the Senate and the courts took no recess at noon, and even there we may believe that, save in times of high excitement, business went on but drowsily. It was during this hour of general repose, which, by the way, was

deemed only less favorable than midnight for the seeing of spectres, that Alaric surprised Rome in the year
410 A.D.

Refreshed by his *merīdiātiō*, the Roman of highly civilized times rose and proceeded directly to **that capital
event of the day, his bath.** The ringing of a bell an-
nounced the opening of the great public baths, *balneae*
or *thermae,* but it does not come within the scope of this
work to describe minutely these characteristic institu-
tions of ancient Rome. They were vast in extent, intri
cate in structure, and enormously costly, and they tended,
as time went on, to become always more and more artistic
and luxurious in their arrangements. Yet the price of
admission, even to the most splendid of these establishments, was so trifling that they were virtually open to
all, — a *quadrāns,* or quarter- *as* (that is to say less than
one cent) for a man, and two for a woman, while children
as a rule were admitted free.

There were usually separate departments for men and
women, but there were porticos and gardens adjoining all
the great *balneae,* where bathers of both sexes might
meet and gossip after the bath was over, as in the casino
of a modern watering-place ; and to the *thermae,* at least,
were often attached libraries and fine art galleries,
*palaestrae* for gymnastic exercise, and *sphaeristēria,* or
courts for playing ball.

The plain, private dwelling of an earlier period had
possessed merely a common *lavātrīna,* or wash-room,
situated near the kitchen for convenience of introducing
both hot and cold water, and where the different members of the family took turns in performing their simple
ablutions. But subsequently, after the bath had come to

be regarded as the greatest of luxuries, it was customary
to have a *balneārium,* or miniature bathing establishment,
somewhat on the plan of the great *balneae,* attached to
every private house, and especially to every country
house having any pretensions to splendor. Traces of
such are to be found all over Europe, wherever the
Roman rule extended, for Roman governors and other
high officials made a point of carrying with them into
their provincial exile the personal habits of the capital.
A private bath of this kind, small but remarkably well

Roman Bath, after a drawing of the 16th century.

preserved, dating from the time of Constantine the Great,
was discovered in 1855, at Caerwent, in Wales, and may
be taken as a type of them all. It was very nearly square
in shape, and its entire dimensions were only thirty-one
Roman feet by thirty-four. The included space was,
however, divided into the usual rooms, or *cellae,* — viz. an
*apodytērium* for undressing, a *tepidārium* provided with
seats for the hot air or vapor bath, a *caldārium* with a
large tub for the hot-water bath, and a *frīgidārium* for
the cold-water bath.

A bather was twice rubbed down by attendant slaves,

once after the vapor or sweating bath, and again after the
cold bath, and after the latter he was also anointed.   In
more elaborate establishments there were separate rooms
for these processes, the *dēstrictārium* and *ūnctōrium*.

The private bath in question was heated on the same
principle as the great *thermae,* that is to say, by means
of a furnace (*hypocaustum, fornāx*) provided with pipes,
through which heated air was conducted underneath the
floors and between the walls of the different rooms.   The
floors were double, the upper one being supported on
pillars of clay piping about two feet high.   The interven-
ing space was made intensely hot, and the whole ingenious arrangement was termed a *suspēnsūra,* and is claimed
by Cicero as the invention of one of his own early friends,
Gaius Sergius Orata.   The heat was graduated for the
different *cellae* by their relative distance from the central
furnace, and the varying thickness of their upper floors.
The *caldārium* was situated nearest the fire, the *apodytērium* farthest from it of the heated rooms, and the succession of hot-air, hot-water, and cold-water baths was
the order regularly observed in bathing establishments of
every grade.

**About an hour after the bath came the** *cēna,* or principal meal of the day.   Once it had been served in the
*ātrium* and had consisted, save upon state occasions,
chiefly of bread or porridge, and vegetables.   The father
and mother and other adult members of the family sat
at table, while children and servants occupied stools or
benches at their feet or behind them.   Long before the
close of the republican period, however, the *cēna,* or
dinner, had developed into as dainty a meal as the
means of the householder would permit; separate din-

ing-rooms were found indispensable in a life of the slightest elegance, and the custom of reclining at table had become universal among the well-to-do. Columella lays it down as a rule that a farm-bailiff should recline at his meals upon high holidays only, and Plutarch, in his life of the younger Cato, tells us that the latter — always a bit of a fanatic — insisted, by way of self-mortification, on *sitting* at table throughout the period of mourning which followed the battle of Pharsalia.

**The ordinary dining-table** was square, surrounded on three sides by the same number of one-armed couches, while the fourth side remained open for convenience of serving. Each of these three couches accommodated three persons, who reclined upon the left arm, supported, the one by the arm of the couch, the other two by heaps of cushions, and always with the feet turned outward. In the assignment of places a strict etiquette prevailed. The couches, or *lecti*, all

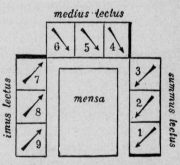

From Kiessling's edition of Horace.

more or less handsomely draped, were distinguished as *medius*, or the one which stood opposite the open side of the table; *summus*, the couch adjoining the head of the *medius;* and *imus*, that upon the other side. The *medius* and the *summus* were assigned to guests; the *imus* accommodated the master of the house, his wife, and one of the elder children or a favorite freedman.

The *medius* was the couch of honor, and the highest place upon it, as also upon the other couches, was the one nearest the arm. The third place, or that at the foot of the *lectus medius*, was, however, called the *locus cōnsulāris*, and was usually assigned to the most important public officer present, both for convenience in the matter of receiving and sending messages and despatches, and because it brought him next the host, who leaned upon the arm of the *īmus*, or lowest couch. Nine was the full number that could be properly served at such a table; a place might be vacant, but to crowd a couch with more than three people was considered the height of vulgarity. Large parties of guests were entertained in spacious dining-halls, or sometimes in summer in the pleasant *sōlāria*, or open *loggie*, on the roofs of the houses, at separate small tables, each accommodating the orthodox number.

**Round tables** with couches fitted so as to form a semi-circle came into fashion in Cicero's time — extravagant objects, for which men paid an insane price. They were made of rare imported woods, preferably from a slab or section of the massive trunk of the so-called citron-tree, a species of African cypress, very beautifully mottled, and the most admired were supported on a single pedestal of solid ivory. Cicero himself had one such for which he paid 500,000 HS. The philosopher Seneca is said to have possessed five hundred. The couches of this luxurious period had often silver feet, and were inlaid with the same precious metal or with ivory and tortoise-shell. The custom had likewise been introduced from the East of hanging the walls of the dining-room with richly embroidered stuffs, and the most sumptuous of all had a very peculiar arrangement of the coffered ceiling. It had long been the fashion to construct this of cross-beams, the square, sunken spaces, or *lacūnāria*, between which were carved, gilded, or otherwise ornamented. These *lacūnāria* were now made in the form of sliding panels, which could be withdrawn for the purpose of scattering flowers, or trifling keepsakes for the guests, upon the table.

*Mantēlia*, or table-cloths, came into use much later than napkins (*mappae*), which last the fashion of eating rendered rather a necessity than a luxury, and they were either brought by the guest or his personal attendant, or offered him by the servants of his host.

The *trīclīniārii*, or dining-room servants, were under the supervision of a *trīclīniārches*, or butler, and the finer the establishment, the more numerous they were. It was their business to arrange the room for the feast, to set forth upon the *abacī*, or sideboards, the imposing array of silver, gold, glass, and jewelled vessels, for both eating and drinking, which would be required in the course of the meal, and accurately to place in the centre of the table its principal ornament, the massive *salīnum*, or salt-cellar. This article, which even the comparatively poor contrived to have made of silver, possessed a certain sacred significance; inasmuch as every table was consecrated to the gods, and the *salīnum* contained not merely salt for seasoning the viands, but a tray (*patella*) for the *molae salsae*, or sacrificial cakes, which were offered to the Lares, and then probably broken and distributed, as a kind of grace, after meat. Silver vessels for vinegar and oil also formed a part of the permanent furniture of every handsome board. The carving and cut-

ting of the meats was done at side-tables; the meal was
served in courses (*fercula*), which were brought in by
the servants on trays (*repositōria*), which had sometimes
two or three shelves or stories, and were presented to the
guests from behind. The wine-cups were replenished in
like manner, "over the shoulder," and these admitted
some variety in form, but were usually shallow, with two
handles, and often very beautiful in workmanship.

The implements actually used in eating were few and
simple, only the right hand
of the guest being free to
wield them. They con-
sisted chiefly of two kinds
of spoons, the *ligula* and
the *cochlear*. The former
was shaped very much like
our own table-spoon, the
latter had a much smaller
bowl, circular in shape, and
flat or only slightly hollowed, and the handle was
pointed for convenience in
detaching the meat of shell-
fish, or picking up particles
of food. Knives and forks

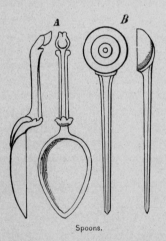

Spoons.

were certainly not employed in Rome as table implements
before the second century of our era.

**A handsome dinner** was served in three principal divisions, each of which might consist of several *fercula*, or
courses. The introductory part was called the *gustus*, or
*gustātiō*, and its object was merely to whet the appetites
of the diners for the richer food to follow. It consisted

mainly of eggs, pickled vegetables, salads in great
variety, oysters, raw or cooked, salted fish, mushrooms,
artichokes, asparagus, or melons, eaten with salt and
pepper. A beverage, *mulsum*, compounded of honey and
must, was often served with the *gustātiō*.

The main part of the meal which followed fell also
into three divisions, — the *prīma*, *altera*, and *tertia cēna*.
It consisted of fish, meats, and game, both native and
foreign, cooked with endless varieties of seasoning, —
salt, pepper, ginger, cinnamon, sweet herbs, and wine.
The fish was usually served with a costly imported sauce
(*garum*), prepared with salt water, of which the flavor
was highly prized. Some of the viands were eaten
steaming hot; others had to be cooled with ice or snow
before they were deemed truly palatable.

There was a pause after this portion of the meal was
concluded, during which the *mola salsa*, already mentioned, was offered to the Lares, after which the *secunda
mēnsa*, or dessert, was brought in. It consisted of pastry,
confectionery, and fruit, both home grown and imported,
and concluded the banquet proper — whence the expression, "*ab ōvō ad māla*," from the egg to the apples,
became proverbial for the whole of anything, from the
beginning to the end.

**Wine was taken in moderation** with all the courses,
rarely clear, sometimes iced, but oftener mixed with
warm water. The business of regular drinking began
only after the dessert had been removed. Those who
affected Greek fashions were now perfumed and crowned
with garlands. The wine was no longer mixed to taste,
in the separate *pōcula* of the guests, but in a huge vase,
or *crātēr*, whence it was ladled out by the servants in

*cyathī*, one-handled cups or ladles. The *cyathus* was the unit of measure for a systematic drinker, who, though he often used a goblet of the capacity of several *cyathī*, always reckoned his feats by the number of the latter which he consumed.

The *cōmissātiō*, or late supper of high-livers, which has been already mentioned, was little more than a drinking-bout. It was enlivened, as was also the *cēna*, by the performance of hired musicians, mimes, and dancers; but conversation, though it found a place, at least in the earlier meal, was never in Rome the fine art and the main entertainment that we find it among the Greeks.

# CHAPTER III.

## CHILDREN, SLAVES, GUESTS, CLIENTS, FREEDMEN.

THE *lūstrātiō*, or naming with religious rites, of a boy infant whom his father had formally acknowledged, occurred on the ninth day after his birth, a girl's upon the eighth. A sacrifice was offered for the child upon the family altar, or it was presented in one or more of the temples of the gods and recommended to their especial protection. As a defence against the evil eye and such mysterious ills, there was also hung round the baby's neck by a ribbon or chain, a small locket, usually heart-shaped or circular, sometimes crescent or cruciform, made of gold if the parents were wealthy, otherwise of some inferior material, and containing an amulet.

This was the *bulla*, of which so many specimens are to be seen in various museums, and which never fails in the picture of a well-born lad. The custom was probably of Etruscan origin, and applied originally to the children of patricians only; but it was subsequently extended to those of knights and of the official nobility generally. A boy wore his *bulla* constantly until he received the gown of manhood; a girl hers until her marriage. But the ornament was always carefully cherished and occasionally resumed, and it is a curious fact that a *triumphātor* invariably put on his *bulla* upon the great day of his public glorification, as a protection against the envy of his fellow-citizens. There was no

Bulla.

such thing as a public registry of births, for civic purposes, before the time of Marcus Aurelius; but a private record of the *lūstrātiō* appears, in most cases, to have been kept, and was sometimes appealed to for purposes of identification.

**The child received its first instruction at home.** Either the mother was the teacher, or, in cases where several married sons lived on under the paternal roof, some freed-woman or female relative of the family acted as nursery governess to all the little ones. In this manner they were taught reading, writing, the elements of arithmetic and of the laws. "When we were boys," says Cicero,[1] "we had to learn the Twelve Tables by heart like a species of hymn. Nobody does it now."

But far more important than even his modicum of book-learning, was held, at least in all the olden time, that practical education which the child received by

[1] Cic. De Leg. ii. 23. 59.

association with his elders, and admission, as he grew older, to their activities.

Thus the girl learned at her mother's side to spin, to weave, and to sew; the boy, of his father or elder brothers, the mysteries of planting and harvesting, swimming, riding, boxing, and the use of weapons. If the father were a *flāmen*, or priest, the son was early trained to assist at sacrifices as his *camillus*, or bearer of the sacred vessels. If the mother offered a sacrifice, her daughter acted as *camilla*. Were the father of a station to receive clients in his *ātrium*, his boys stood beside him during the ceremony, and so learned to know the names and faces of his political and social following. On days of family triumph or mourning, when the shrines were opened, and the images of the ancestors displayed, the children were always present. They took part in the family meals, when these were simple and there were no guests, and sometimes they helped serve at table.

Very early also in the history of Rome we find mention of both boys' and girls' schools. Plutarch seems to imply that even Romulus and Remus went to school at Gabii, and the unhappy Virginia was on her way to school when her precocious beauty attracted the fatal notice of Appius Claudius. Virginia was, however, of plebeian rank, and her mother was dead.

**The primary teacher** (*lītterātor*) was usually a slave or freedman, who acted as private tutor, or instructed a small class in the *pergula*, or veranda attached to a house or shop. Schooling of this kind was paid for by the month, occasionally by the year, and very poorly paid; insomuch that the *lītterātor* had often to eke out his income by some other employment, such as the writing of wills. Under Diocletian the monthly fees of a pupil were limited to fifty *dēnāriī*.[1]

The school year consisted of eight months, with a long vacation comprising July, August, September, and October. There were also special holidays, such as the feast of Minerva, and the Sāturnālia, New Year's Day, and the twenty-second of February, the great day of commemoration of the dead.

The substance of what was taught in these primary schools was the same as that which an old-fashioned or more carefully secluded child acquired at home, — reading, writing, and the elements of arithmetic, while the laws of the Twelve Tables, as we have already seen, were long committed to memory like a sort of catechism.

The Roman system of numerals, in which values are expressed by the collocation of different letters of the alphabet, appears, beside the simplicity of the Arabic, a very clumsy one; and the regular employment of duodecimal fractions, or division of the unit into twelfths, increased yet more the difficulties of reckoning. We are not surprised therefore to learn that even grown men often had recourse to a teacher of arithmetic, or *calculātor*, who was much better paid than the common schoolmaster, nor that the boy at his desk was allowed to assist his ciphering by using the fingers of both hands, as well as by the *abacus*, or counting-machine.

Reckoning with the fingers, not yet wholly disused in the East, proceeded upon the basis of expressing by

[1] It is not exactly known what a *dēnārius* was worth under Diocletian. Mommsen computes it at nine German *pfennige*, which would make this maximum monthly price about one dollar.

eighteen different motions of the left hand, nine units and nine tens, and, by similar movements of the right hand, nine hundreds and nine thousands. The term *abacus*, which we have already seen applied to the side-table of a dining-room, was also used both for a board strewn with sand, on which

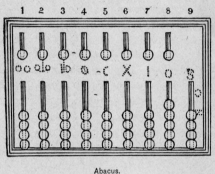

Abacus.

geometrical figures were drawn with a pointed stick, or *stilus*, and for one on which balls representing figures were moved about in grooves representing denominations of figures. This kind of *abacus* had also a contrivance for reckoning fractions.

The Roman monetary system had practically two units of value, the *sēstertius* and its quadruple, the *dēnārius*. Large sums were commonly computed in the former and reckoned by a decimal system. Small sums were expressed in the latter and its duodecimal fractions. The difficulty which must have arisen from the simultaneous use of the decimal and duodecimal systems was diminished by rules and tables for reducing the one kind of fraction to the other, and these rules and tables apparently found a place in the curriculum of the elementary schools.

The simple instruction, purely practical in its aim, of these primitive establishments was deemed all-sufficient

for the youth of Rome down to the time of the second
Punic war. But after that period there grew up an ever-
increasing demand for the services of Greek gramma-
rians, who not only taught their own language, but introduced a more scientific method of studying the Latin
itself; and who succeeded, after a time, in imbuing the
Roman mind with something resembling the broad ideal
of Greek culture, — that is to say, of the harmonious and
equal development of all a man's faculties, both physical
and mental.

**The principal text-book** of the Greek *grammaticus* was
Homer. The master read aloud, with proper accent and
inflection, a passage from the poet. This the pupil had
first to commit to memory, and afterward to stand a certain examination, not merely upon its grammar and
prosody, but on all the various questions in geography,
astronomy, history, and mythology which it might sug-
gest. Written exercises had also to be prepared, trans-
lations from poetry into prose, and original themes.

The criticism of these last must have involved some
elementary teaching in rhetoric, but a further pursuit of
the various branches of learning comprehended under
this head was reserved for the higher schools of the
rhetoricians.

The grammatical course was deemed equally appropriate for boys and girls, and a good number of the latter
attended the grammar schools; although there was
plainly always a prejudice in favor of home education
for them.

To get the full benefit even of this amount of instruction it was needful that the pupil should both understand
and speak Greek, and this the children of the wealthy

learned to do in infancy from domestic slaves of that nation, as those of the Russian nobility learn French and English from their nursery governesses to-day.

As soon as a boy was old enough to **begin his public education,** he was placed under the special charge of a servant, called *paedagōgus,* whose business it was to help him prepare his lessons, and go with him to school, and who continued to be his personal attendant until he received the *toga virīlis.*

Long after this period a young man might, and often did, frequent the schools of rhetoric, which, like the grammar schools, were an importation from Greece, and conducted mainly upon the Greek method, and where music and the higher mathematics were taught, as well as the arts of composition and oratory.

Yet it is evident that a dull but deep-seated objection to all this outlandish culture lingered throughout the whole republican period, not merely among the masses, but in the minds of enthusiasts for the old Roman spirit and traditions, like the elder Cato; and when Atticus, the friend of Cicero, published a collection of Greek anecdotes, we find Lucullus congratulating him upon the barbarism of some of his expressions, on the ground that it did not become a good Roman to know Greek too well.

After the Romans came to have a literature of their own, there grew up a class of *grammaticī Latīnī,* who made a business of teaching Terence, Horace, and Virgil, and who were much frequented. The corresponding class of Latin *rhētorēs* had never found favor, either with individuals or with the state. Their teaching was of a very inferior order, and their influence upon manners was considered so bad that as early as the year 92 B.C. all such Latin schools of rhetoric were closed by order of the Censors, Domitius and Cassius.

Every well-bred Roman boy learned to ride, to run, to leap, to box, and to swim, as a necessary preparation for his military service, and the Campus Martius was assigned for the practice of these and all other athletic exercises.

Under ordinary circumstances a lad was supposed to have finished his regular schooling by the end of his seventeenth year, at which time also he ceased to be *puer* and became *iuvenis*, and liable for military duty. Already, in the vast majority of cases, he had laid aside the *toga praetexta*, or simple woollen tunic with a broad purple stripe (*clāvus lātus*) down the front, worn by both boys and girls of rank, and had been ceremoniously invested by his father or guardian with the *toga virīlis*, or *toga pūra*, the plain white garment of manhood. No precise age was fixed for this solemnity, and the time of the year was also optional, although the religious feast of the *Līberālia* — March 17th — was undoubtedly a favorite season. The *bulla* was first removed from the boy's neck and consecrated to the *Larēs*, and an offering was then made for him in the family chapel, after which, accompanied by a train of relatives and friends, he was led into the Forum and formerly presented to the public. His full name was afterwards inscribed in the list of citizens kept in the *Tabulārium* upon the Capitol, or among the archives of his province; a sacrifice was offered for him at some public altar, and a banquet followed, accompanied, in the case of imperial and other very distinguished youth, by

granted that such philanthropists were not exceptionally numerous in ancient Rome.

**The modest corps of house servants** maintained by a distinguished Roman in the earlier time was headed by an *ātriēnsis*, or steward, who also kept the house-accounts. Later, as the style of living grew more elaborate, these duties had to be divided, and the *ātriēnsis* became a mere major-domo, who had enough to do in exercising a general supervision over the arrangements of the dwelling itself. The ever-increasing crowd of menials under him fell into different classes, each with an overseer of its own. The *cubiculāriī* performed the duties of housemaids, the *triclīnāriī* waited at table, the *supellēctāriī* kept the furniture and table-ware in order, the *culīnāriī* were kitchen drudges, while the *balneāriī*, or those who served the baths, formed another distinct class. The functions of valet and ladies' maid were distributed amongst *ōrnā-tōrēs* and *ōrnātrīcēs*, *tōnsōrēs*, or barbers, and *ciniflōnēs*, or hair-crimpers, and *calceātōrēs* who took care of the feet. There were *dēlicātī*, or pages, more or less pampered, to run on errands, an *invītātor* to summon guests, a *servus ab hospitiīs* to look after their lodgement, a porter (*iāni-tor* or *ōstiārius*) who was sometimes chained in the vesti-bule like a dog. Were the master of an artistic or literary turn, he had people whose special duty it was to look after his pictures and statues, — servants *ā pinacothēcā* and *ā statuīs*,— *tabellāriī* to convey his letters to their destination, *lectōrēs* to read aloud to him at meals, in the bath, or in bed.

The number of slaves who should accompany a great man or a great lady when he or she went abroad, was matter of lively emulation. Those who walked had *ante-*

*ambulātōrēs,* and *pedīsequī* or *pedisequae* to go before and
behind them.  If they took the air in litters, they were
borne by *lectārii,* the most fashionable being Syrians or
Cappadocians of unusual stature, who, like the pages,
wore a brilliant livery.  The boy, as we have seen, had
his *paedagōgus* to attend him to school, the daughter of
well-to-do parents had her Greek maid, who performed
the same office.  There was often a *capsārius* besides to
carry the books and tablets.

All these functionaries were slaves, a limited number
being of the comparatively privileged servile class called
*vernae;* that is to say, slaves born in the house and usually trained for the personal service of its children, many
of whose educational and other privileges they shared.
The freedman who had been *verna,* always held himself
superior to other manumitted slaves.

A highly prized slave was occasionally set free, by
pure grace, or in gratitude for some signal service,
either during the lifetime of his master, or in his will.
The right of the slave to his own small savings ( *pecū-
lium*) was also practically recognized and these might
be applied to the purchase of his freedom; but their
accumulation, very slow at best, was yet farther hin-
dered by the master's claim upon the little horde, for
making good certain pecuniary injuries which he might
sustain through the slave.  After the number of bondmen
had increased enormously, so that one man sometimes
owned many thousand souls, it became advantageous for
the master to educate them wholesale in trades and crafts
for which they might show some aptitude, and then let
them out to master-mechanics, bankers, seamen, theatrical managers, or masters of the amphitheatre, as the
case might be.

Sometimes, too, the master directly advanced the capital for setting his slave up in business, allowing the latter a share of the profits, out of which he might hope some day to buy his freedom.

**The common punishment of a refractory slave** was beating. If a runaway were caught, as he could hardly fail to be, since there were extremely heavy penalties for harboring and assisting him, he was either branded or had an iron collar like a dog's welded round his neck, or his legs were fettered, or in exaggerated or repeated cases of offence he was at once turned into the arena or otherwise put to death. If he attempted to take personal vengeance upon his master for any wrong whatsoever, his whole family shared his fate, and the regular form of capital punishment for a slave was crucifixion under the most ignominious and agonizing circumstances.

The institution of slavery reached its greatest development in Rome in the last century of the republic, when slave-traders and slave-markets flourished both in the capital itself, and in all the great ports visited by Roman ships.

Already, however, in the early days of the empire, the spread of philosophic and humanitarian ideas had softened the theory of human servitude, and modified the slave's position. Marriage was made legal for him; he was empowered to testify in certain courts, and to lodge complaint, if treated with outrageous cruelty. Kind masters, like Pliny, respected the provisions of his testament; under Claudius, if his master abandoned him when he was old or ill, he was thereby set free; under Hadrian, the wanton slaughter of a slave by his master was forbidden; under Constantine, this crime was made one of homicide; and so finally, with the formal conversion of the empire to Christianity, the long-declining slave-system of Rome received its death-blow.

We have considered briefly the position and mutual relations of the ordinary members of a Roman household, or of what may be called the inner family circle; but there was a sense in which the Roman family might be said to embrace an indefinitely larger number of persons connected with it by ties more or less remote. To this outer circle, or secondary order of members, belonged the authorized guests of a house, its clients, and its freedmen.

**The term hospitium** embraced not merely the spontaneous welcome to bed and board of a man's near kindred and personal friends, but a contract for mutual hospitality, written or otherwise attested, which might be made either between two communities, or between two individuals, on behalf of themselves and their dependents, or between an individual and a community. The practice was one of extreme antiquity in Italy, older certainly than the rise of the Roman people. The contract was drawn up and presented by accredited messengers, attested by a hand-shake or by a formula of words called the *sponsiō*, and accurately recorded, and it remained binding upon the posterity of the contracting parties until formally and publicly annulled.

*Hospitium* between two communities, that is, between the inhabitants of certain towns or districts, was called *hospitium pūblicum*. It was recorded by engraving on copper or bronze tablets,[1] of which duplicate copies were

[1] It seems altogether probable that a part at least of the famous Eugubean tables — the bronze tablets exquisitely engraved in ar-

preserved in some temple, or other sacred place, in either town. In Rome the depository of such tablets was the *Aedēs fideī populī Rōmānī*.

They entitled the stranger to free board and lodging for a certain period, to a physician's attendance in illness, to decent burial if he died.

Such contracts were in force between Roman and Greek communities as well, and they involved no light charge upon the latter in the days when foreign travel had become a fashion among the Roman magnates. But some — like Cicero when he went as proconsul to Cilicia — preferred to remain independent, and would not avail themselves of the privileges of a public guest.

*Hospitia prīvāta*, or contracts for hospitality between individuals, were also sometimes engraved and either inserted in the wall of the *ātrium* or suspended on it. Usually, however, a simpler device was employed by private persons. The guest presented a small engraved ticket (*tessera*), of which the host had a duplicate, and was at once made welcome to the privileges of the house. He was given a bath and a meal; an offering was made for him at the family altar; he was assigned a bed, and became thenceforth, for an indefinite period, a member of the family. So far from fretting under this as an imposition, the great Roman statesman was ambitious of harboring as many such guests as possible, and it was a matter of policy with him to look well after their comfort and interests on the ground that they increased his own influence in the provinces and abroad.

chaic and hitherto only partially deciphered characters — discovered under the ruins of an ante-Roman theatre, and now preserved in the *palazzo pubblico* of Gubbio in the Marches, were records of *hospitia pūblica*, dating from Etruscan or even Pelasgic times.

Originally, and so long as the state remained free, **the relation of client and patron** was also a sufficiently honorable one, resting like that of guest and host, on pledges of mutual service. There was this difference, however, between the position of a client and that of a legal guest, that the latter was a free citizen in his own community, while the former had usually no civic rights whatever. Either he was in banishment from his native place, or he belonged to a tribe or city which had been vanquished in war, and so disfranchised; or he was a freedman (*libertus*) whose manumission gave him no political status. In either case he needed the protection of some powerful personage, and was only too glad, in return for the same, to take the name of his patron, engaging to fight his battles both at home and abroad, and to assist him out of his own private means — if he had such — when extraordinary payments, as of ransom or dowry, were to be made, or the patron was in any way pressed for money. Clients and patrons might neither accuse nor testify against one another in the courts, and the laws of the Twelve Tables made it a capital offence for a patron to betray his client's interests. It was no uncommon thing for the entire population of conquered cities and states voluntarily to seek such a relation with the general who had subdued them, and with his descendants. Thus the Marcelli became the hereditary patrons of the Sicilian towns, the Fabii of the Allobrogian, Cato Uticensis of the island of Cyprus, and so on. The freedman either continued to reside in his patron's house and perform his old functions, or he was endowed by the latter with a capital for starting in business, or with some small freehold property. In case of subsequent impoverishment, they were still bound to assist one another. The patron always paid for the funeral of his freedman, was his legal heir if he died childless, and the *ex officiō* guardian of his children if he left any under age.

**The relations of patron and libertus** remained virtually the same throughout the imperial period; those of patron and client, on the other hand, altered materially, and, from a moral point of view, very much for the worse. When the number and strength of a patron's following had ceased to have any political significance, and no longer increased his importance in the state, it became largely a matter of senseless ostentation on the one side, and of self-interested sycophancy on the other. The hangers-on of a great man received their maintenance, and this, in most instances, was all they wanted. They were of every rank and condition, men of letters from whom a certain tribute was expected in the way of flattery, soldiers of fortune, and professional legacy-hunters, scions of the great families, who had early run through their patrimony, the idle of every grade, with a tatterdemalion fringe of the congenitally and hopelessly poor. A few favored individuals out of this motley regiment might be invited to the patron's own table, but all claimed as their right, and regularly received, either one substantial meal in a day, or its equivalent in money. Occasionally the mass of the clients was regaled at a public feast (*epulum pūblicum*), where the viands were supplied by a contractor (*manceps*) at so much a head. This was called a *cēna rēcta*, and was, originally, at least an exceptional arrangement, for days of public celebration; as when Julius Cæsar,

on the occasion of his triumph, in 56 B.C., entertained
the entire male population of Rome at 22,000 *triclīnia*.
A more common custom was to appoint a place where
a species of dole was distributed to all the *clientèle*.
This practice was called *epulum dividere*, and the dole
itself *sportula* from the basket in which the food was
taken away; the same name being applied in imperial
times to the small money-payment, which had now uni-
versally replaced the alms in kind.   The average amount
of this daily allowance, under the earlier emperors, was
twenty-five *assēs*, or about thirty-three cents of our
money.   On special occasions, like the patron's birthday, a larger sum was given.   Martial[1] mentions one
such where it was trebled, but adds contemptuously that
it was doubtful whether the man had a right to any
birthday at all.   On the other hand if the great man
were ill and could not receive his clients, there appears
to have been no distribution; but even so, a client who
managed to make a number of successive salutations,
and to keep well with several patrons, as many did,
might secure, without further exertion, a modest maintenance for a rising family.

[1] Mar. Epig. x. 27.

# CHAPTER IV.

## FOOD AND CLOTHING.

BREAD, wine, and oil, — on these three abundant and beautiful products of the Italian peninsula the mass of its inhabitants lived and throve in ancient times as they do to-day. Wheat was the grain most grown by the Romans, and wheaten porridge or bread their staple food. In very ancient times the grain of wheat was not even ground, but merely pounded in a mortar, mixed with water, and cooked to the consistency of a thick pulp, called *puls*. The slaves who pounded the grain were *pīstōrēs*, or *pīnsitōrēs*. Even after the superiority of baked bread had been discovered, the baking continued for a long time to be done at home, and was regarded as the special business of the house-mother, or of the chief cook, according to the rank and means of the family. The first public bakery of Rome was established in 171 B.C., after which time home-made bread went gradually out of use in cities, though it had still to be prepared on rural estates by slaves appointed for the purpose. Later it became one of the recognized functions of the general government (it had long been held such in times of scarcity) to regulate, year by year, the food supply of the nation; and to see that the mass of the people was provided with cheap and wholesome bread.  The bread-makers of Rome were now organized into a college or guild, under the presidency of the *Praefectus Annōnae*, and vast establishments, comprising both mills and bakeries, were built and let out to them by the State.

The members of this guild enjoyed special privileges and immunities, which were extended, after the general decline of agriculture, when grain had to be imported in vast quantities, to the ship-owner and seamen (*nāviculāriī* and *caudicāriī*), on whose enterprise the supply of bread-stuffs largely depended.  Trajan, we are told,[1] gave the *ius suffrāgiī* to every man who had worked for three years a *pīstrīnum* (grain-mill) in which at least one hundred *modiī* of corn had been ground daily.  But it must always be remembered that even under that excellent emperor the suffrage did not mean what it had done when the state was free.

As early as the times of the Gracchi (130 B.C.) there had been a monthly distribution of grain among the people.  Four hundred years later, under the Emperor Aurelian, there had come to be a daily distribution of baked bread, either gratuitous or at a nominal price, with which, and the perpetual exhibition of games in the Circus (*"pānem et Circēnsēs"*), the Roman burgher of those degenerate days found his absolute needs both of body and mind satisfied without further exertion upon his own part.

Different qualities of bread were provided even at the great public bakeries.  The best was the *pānis silīgineus*, made from *silīgo*, or wheat flour of the very first quality ; the *simila* or *similāgo* was also a fine white flour, only a

---

[1] Gaii. Inst. 1. 34.

little inferior to the first. Coarser varieties of bread, — the *pānis cibārius, plēbēius, rūsticus,* as also the *pānis castrēnsis,* or bread of the common soldier, — were made by mixing flour of the second quality with bran, or wholly of bran, or sometimes of inferior grains like millet.

Besides the great public magazines of bread, there were many small cake-shops, where cakes, pastry, and confectionery, and, in general, all the dainties which are summed up by the modern Italian under the comprehensive term *dolci* (sweets) were made and sold. But these establishments were conducted by private enterprise, and their keepers were *dulciārii placentārii, lībārii, crūstulārii,* as the case might be. These were the shops which we have already seen besieged by the school-boys in the early morning hours; but the choice of the young students was probably limited, and they had to content themselves for the most part, no doubt, with the harmless *quadra pānis,* a plain, round cake quartered off by two lines like a hot-cross bun, of which plenty of illustrations

Panis (Rich).

exist, and of which specimens were found at Pompeii.

**The grain-mills** of the ancients were of three kinds, the *molae manuāriae,* or hand-mills, the *molae asināriae,* turned by asses or mules, and the *molae aquāriae,* or water-mills. The first two were identical in principle, and differed only in size. They consisted of two parts, the *mēta,* or nether, and the *catīllus,* or upper mill-stone; but their construction was very unlike that of the mills of modern times. The *mēta* was a solid cone of stone resting upon a firm base with an iron rod projecting a little way from its apex. The *catīllus* consisted of two hollow stones, united in the form of an hour-glass. The lower half fitted over the cone of the *mēta* like an inverted cup. It had a socket at the narrowest part,

Mola (Rich).

which received the rod aforesaid, and was made to revolve upon it by means of a projecting handle or lever. The grain was poured into the upper cup, and falling between the lower and the solid cone through holes bored for the purpose, it was ground by the revolution of the *catīllus*. If the mill were large and worked by horse-power, there was only one lever, to which the animal, whose eyes had first been bandaged to prevent its becoming dizzy, was harnessed. The smaller hand-mills had a lever projecting on either side, and were worked by two slaves. Water-mills did not come into general use in Rome before the fourth century of our era, when there was a group of such at the foot of the Janiculan hill. The actual machinery for grinding was still substantially the same as that already described, but the power was now supplied by streams of water falling from an artificial reservoir at the top of the hill upon a large water-wheel (*rota aquāria*) with float-boards, and having attached to its axis a pair of cog-wheels (*tympana dentāta*) whose motion turned the *catīllus*. It was that able and resourceful general, Belisarius, who, during the siege of Rome by the Goths in 536, devised a system of floating corn-mills, whose wheels were turned by the current of the Tiber somewhat like those which may be seen in such numbers upon the Danube to-day between Vienna and Buda-Pesth.

Bacon and the sweet, nutty oil of the country were used to impart a relish to porridge and coarse bread, and the ordinary drink of the peasant was milk or must, the unfermented juice of the grape. Moreover, even the comparatively poor man had access to an almost infinite variety of vegetables, — beans, peas, lentils, cabbages, beets, turnips, radishes, carrots, asparagus, artichokes, chiccory, onions, leeks, garlic and parsley, melons and cucumbers. Lettuce, mallow, cress, and many other plants were largely cultivated for salads; and for seasoning, mustard, anise, fennel, mint, and so on.

Beans and onions were the vegetables most extensively raised in ancient times, the name of the Fabian gens and the cognomen Cæpio being derived from these crops. Beans, however, — forbidden altogether by Pythagoras to his disciples, — were considered too heavy food for any but smiths, gladiators, and farm hands; and though Varro maintains that the men of old were at their raciest when their talk smelt of onions and garlic, the taste for these fierce condiments declined fast with the progress of refinement; insomuch that Horace devotes an entire epode (the third) to his execration of the latter, and Nævius reproaches the gods for not having confounded the gardener who first grew an onion. The finest of all vegetables to the elder Cato was cabbage, which seems quite consistent with what we know of his character.

The natural fruits of Italy, apples, pears, plums,

quinces, olives, and grapes, were carefully cultivated from very early times, and Lucretius, Varro, and Virgil agree in describing the land as literally covered with vineyards and orchards : " *tōta pōmārium,*" says Varro. These common fruits were cheap enough in their due season, and found a place upon almost every table ; but as luxury increased, there came to be great emulation on the part of the horticulturists in the forcing of early fruit, in the production of new varieties, which were often, then as now, called after distinguished men, as the Matian apple for Gaius Matius, and the Appian from an Appius Claudius ; and lastly in the introduction and naturalization of foreign fruits, as the pomegranate (*grānātum*) from Carthage, the fig and almond (*ficus, amȳgdala*) from Greece, the peach (*mālum Persicum*) from Persia, the apricot (*mālum Armeniacum*) from Armenia, the pistaccio nut (*pistāchium*), unknown before the time of Tiberius, and many others.

Dried figs, dates, and damson-plums were largely imported, and both the native and the naturalized fruits of Italy were introduced by Roman colonists into far distant provinces, as the cherry (*cerasum*) into Britain and the pistachio (*pistāchium*) into Spain.

**The diet of the early Roman,** though never exclusively vegetarian, appears to have been about as largely so as that of the Italian peasant of to-day. The slaughter of neat cattle for food was long regarded as a crime ; mutton, pork, and goat's flesh were the meats most in use. As time went on and taste became more sophisticated, the craving for animal food increased, and accomplished cooks like him in the Pseudolus of Plautus came to regard vegetables as merely accessories to it, and fitter upon the whole for the nourishment of animals than men.

The taste for game also developed rapidly, until the sportsman's bag no longer sufficed for its gratification, but all great country-seats in the last years of the republic had their *vivāria*, or preserves. The kinds of wild flesh most esteemed were hare (*lepus*), wild-goat (*caper*), though this was condemned by Galen as unwholesome, the wild boar (*aper*), which was roasted whole and so served at sumptuous tables, and even the wild ass (*onager*), and a certain species of dormouse (*glis*).

Over and above the ordinary kinds of domestic fowl, feathered game was also in great request, such as the *lagōpūs* or white grouse, the *scolōpax* or snipe, the *attagēn Iōnicus* or woodcock, which was considered a marvellous delicacy, besides thrushes (*turdī*), partridges (*perdīcēs*), ortolans (*miliāriae*), pheasants (*phāsiānī*), cranes (*gruēs*), and *pāvōnēs*, or peacocks. These last indeed seem to have been regarded in the year 46 B.C. as the *ne plus ultra* of table luxury in this line, for it was then that Cicero wrote to his old friend Papirius Pætus, concerning the banquets to which he was perpetually bidden by certain young men of fashion, "whom he taught to declaim, while they taught him to dine,"[1] that he had "eaten more peacocks"[2] that winter than Pætus had "ever eaten pigeons." And a little later he tells how he endeavored to pay off his obligations by a handsome dinner to the same set of youths. "However," he adds, "I did not attempt to have peacock."[3]

**For fish there seems to have been no demand** whatever in early Roman times, although the taste for it subsequently grew, as artificial tastes are wont to do, into a passion;

[1] Cic. Ad Fam. ix. 16.     [2] Cic. Ad Fam. ix. 18.
[3] Cic. Ad Fam. ix. 20.

so that the word *obsōnium*, originally applied to any
kind of cooked food except bread, came to signify fish
exclusively. Already, in the elder Cato's time, fish was
dearer than beef; unheard-of sums were paid to import
alive the fish of other countries, and fish-tanks and fish-
ponds (*piscīnae*) for the cultivation of choice varieties
became one of the favorite extravagancies of the wealthy.
Among the most prized of the native species were the
*acipēnser*, a kind of sturgeon; the *asellus*, which seems to
have resembled our cod; *lupus*, a species of pike, so
named from its voracity, but of which those only were
approved by epicures which were taken in the Tiber, —
*inter duōs pontēs* — that is, in the neighborhood of the
island; the *mŭllus*, or mullet, especially the bearded
mullet, which, though seldom weighing more than two
Roman pounds, often fetched an enormous price; the
*rhombus*, a kind of turbot; and later, the river-fish of
North Italy, of the Danube, the Rhine, and the Moselle.
There was, moreover, a vast importation of different
kinds of salted and pickled fish from various Mediterranean ports, those which came from Spain, Sardinia,
and Pontus being most esteemed. The common name
for all these preparations was *tarĭchos*, a word borrowed
from the Greek, and under this head were comprised
many different sorts and grades. There was *tarĭchos*
made from fat fishes and *tarĭchos* made from lean; there
was a delicate variety made entirely from the young fry
taken in the spring, and a coarser but still highly appe-
tizing kind made from the large slices (*Melandrya*) cut
from the back of the *thunnus*, or tunny-fish; first salted
and dried in the sun, then cooked in sea-water or oil, and
eaten with vinegar and mustard, by way of *gustātōrium*,
at the beginning of a meal.

Salted fish was of course a cheaper food than fresh, and there was a certain savory dish, the *tyrotarichus*, made of some kind of *tarichos*, eggs and cheese, or spices, which was the subject of endless jests between Cicero and his friends, as a kind of symbol of resolute frugality.

**Oysters** (*ostreae*) were considered as great a delicacy in Roman times as now. Imported in the first instance from the East, and especially from Abydos, they came to be extensively cultivated in the neighborhood of Naples, especially in the Avernine and Lucrine lakes, and subsequently in the remotest parts of the western provinces. In the time of Ausonius, the oysters of Burdigala (Bordeaux) in Gaul were particularly relished. An important industry also grew up out of the manufacture, in seaport towns, of three kinds of fish-sauce, *garum*, *muria*, and *allex*, which greatly tickled the sophisticated Roman palate. *Garum* was made chiefly from sturgeon or mackerel; *muria* from tunny. Their preparation is not perfectly understood, but in both cases the fish appears to have been slightly cooked in sea-water, and allowed to ferment for several months. The resultant mixture was then strained, and the clear liquor, which was very costly, constituted *garum* or *muria*, the residuum *allex*. The word *muria* was also used for any brine, and there was a cheap sort of *allex*, home-made from ordinary fish, which was given to slaves as a relish with their porridge.

**Sugar and butter** were unknown among the Romans, their place being supplied by honey and oil.

**A few words only need be given in this place to the comprehensive subjects of oil and wine;** since the mode of manufacturing, from the olive and the grape, these important articles, or at least accessories of a Roman diet, will be fully described in the chapter on Agriculture. The cultivation of the olive for oil was as old in Italy as the time of the Tarquins. It spread thence to Gaul and to Spain; but the Italian oils were always considered the best in the world, and they were profitably exported in ancient times, as they are to-day. **The vine was native all over the peninsula,** and always esteemed a pecul-iarly sacred product of the soil. It was under the direct patronage of Jove, in whose honor were celebrated, on the twenty-third of April and the twentieth of August, the feasts of the *Vīnālia Urbāna* and the *Vīnālia Rūstica;* and the vintage was opened by the *flāmen diālis* with a religious ceremony. These pious, old-fashioned customs, however, had reference merely to the production of the ordinary sour wines of the country, like Horace's *vīle Sabīnum*, or that acrid wine of the Alban Mount, which excited the merriment of Cineas, the ambassador of Pyr-rhus.[1] The careful and expensive culture of the vine for the production of choice local varieties did not begin in Italy until after that of cereals had notably declined.

The elder Pliny tells us in his Natural History,[2] that at the time of his writing, which was probably about 50 A.D., there were some eighty varieties of good wine in the Roman market, of which number nearly two-thirds were grown in Italy. Excellent kinds were raised, on all the southern slopes of the Alban hills, at Velitræ, at Præneste, and notably at Formiæ upon the coast. Among the Sabine wines, the once renowned Cæcuban, which Augustus considered the noblest wine on earth, and which chiefly came from the neighborhood of Terra-

[1] Plin. Nat. Hist. xiv. 3.      [2] Plin. Nat. Hist. xiv. 11.

cina, was no longer grown in Pliny's time, and its name
had become a kind of general expression for any particularly excellent vintage. The yet more famous Falernian
in all its varieties, brown and pale, sweet and dry, had
also lost something of its prestige, owing to the fact
that it was unscrupulously adulterated. But the product of the Mons Massicus, so often and melodiously
praised both by Horace and Virgil, still held its pre-
eminent place among the wines of the South, and fine
varieties were grown upon Vesuvius, in all the environs
of Naples and Pompeii, at Cumæ, and at Sorrento. The
wine of the latter place was much recommended by physicians, but it took twenty-five years to ripen, and Tiberius
called it "a noble vinegar." There was a brisk demand
for certain Sicilian wines, especially those of Messala,
Taormina, and Syracuse, and also for those of Central and
Eastern Italy, from the vineyards about Spoleto, Ancona,
and Cesena, near Ravenna, where, indeed, wine was not
merely more wholesome, but cheaper than water. From
Aquileia in the North came the *Vinum Pūcīnum*, to the
use of which Livia ascribed her eighty-two years of exceptional health, and the excellent wine of Istria. The
Tuscan wines, as a whole, were considered inferior; the
best was that which came from the higher levels of
the Mediterranean coast, near the white marble city of
Lūna. The Rhætic wine of Verona was particularly
esteemed among those of Cisalpine Gaul.

Wines of Spain, Provence, the Mediterranean islands,
Greece, and Asia Minor, were always to be found in the
Roman market, but those of the East were always prepared for transportation by a treatment with sea-water
and resin. Wines which ripened slowly, as those of the

far South almost always do, were often taken when unfermented, and either cooked or exposed to the sun or
the action of smoke ; and there were Gallic wines, which,
like the Scotch whiskey of to-day, always retained a
peculiar flavor due to the latter process.

Among the cheaper fermented drinks relished by the
Romans were cider, perry, date and mulberry wines.

Mention has already been made of the beverage called
*mulsum*, which was compounded principally of wine and
honey, and sipped at the beginning of a meal; but other
condiments were added to this mixture in almost infinite
variety ; a species of mulse flavored with pepper, and
hence called *pipperātum*, was a special favorite, while
more than fifty kinds of distilled liqueurs were manufactured from the juices of different aromatic plants.

----

**The first thing to be noted about the dress of the Romans**
is that its prevalent material was always woollen.  Sheep-
raising for wool was practised among them on an extensive scale, from the earliest historic times, and the
choice breeds of that animal, originally imported from
Greece or Asia Minor, took so kindly to the soil and
climate of Italy that home-grown wool came even to be
preferred to the foreign for fineness and softness of
quality.   Foreign wools were, however, always imported
more or less, partly because the supply of native wools
seems never to have been quite sufficient, partly because
the natural colors of wools from different parts varied
so considerably as to render the art of the dyer to some
extent unnecessary.   Thus, the wools of Canusium (Can-
ossa) were brown or reddish, those of Pollentia in

Liguria were black, those from the Spanish Bætica, which comprised Andalusia and a part of Granada, had either a golden-brown or a grayish hue; the wools of Asia were almost all red; and there was a Grecian fleece, called the crow-colored, of which the natural tint was a peculiarly deep and brilliant black.

**Goats' wool** was rarely used for articles of clothing. Peasants, and especially shepherds, wrapped themselves in goat-skins, as they still do; but only the wool of the long-haired foreign varieties from Spain, Africa, and Asia Minor [1] was regularly woven into rough and heavy cloths, which were used for tent-coverings, for bagging in commerce, for blankets and warm overshoes, and to protect the outer walls of houses in stormy weather against the wind and rain. Ropes and cables were also made of goats' hair.

**Linen cloth** made from the fibre of flax was undoubtedly an Egyptian invention; but the cultivation of the plant was ancient all over Italy, as well as the weaving of home-spun linen fabrics, for the undergarments both of men and women, and the belts and girdles of the latter, for the bandages needed in medical practice, and the awnings (*vēla*) which were used as a protection from the sun. Linen threads were also made, and cords for hunting and fishing-nets. The finer grades of woven linen required in later and more luxurious times for handkerchiefs, table-cloths, napkins, and bedding, and, finally, for entire suits of garments, were always manufactured abroad, especially at Damascus, Laodicea, Tarsus, and Alexandria; and the later Emperors had private

[1] The hair-shirt of later times, *cilicium*, got its name from the Cilician goat.

linen factories both in the East and at Vienna (Vienne
in France), where imperial slaves were kept at work to
supply the requirements of the court.

**Cotton and cotton fabrics** came always from the far
East. Introduced into Greece by the returning soldiers
of Alexander the Great, late in the fourth century B.C.,
they were certainly known in Rome not much more than
a hundred years afterwards, for we find the word
*carbasina* applied to a stuff by the comic poet Cæcilius
Statius in 191 B.C.; now *carbasus* was the technical
word for Indian muslin, and it is identical with the
Sanscrit name (*karpâsî*) of the cotton-plant. The term
was no doubt often loosely employed by Roman writers
for linen as well as cotton fabrics; but the latter had the
great advantage for the ancients of receiving more readily the blue and purple dyes which they specially affected,
and they came on this account to be even preferred by
many for purposes of personal adornment.

**Silk** (*sericum*), too, was an article of Eastern luxury,
and hardly known in Rome before the end of the republic. The Roman soldiers had indeed seen in 54 B.C. the
fluttering of silken banners wrought with gold, and borne
before the advancing Parthians; but not until the time
of Augustus do we find frequent mention of silken garments, of which three varieties are distinguished, — the
*vestēs Coae*, the *vestēs bombȳcinae*, and the *vestēs sēricae*.
The Coan robes were extremely costly, transparently
fine and thin in texture, purple in color, and usually embroidered with gold. They came from the cocoon of the
Chinese worm, and derived their name from the Ægean
island, where the silken yarn was spun, dyed, and woven.
The *vestēs bombȳcinae* came chiefly from Assyria, where

the native silk was yellowish in color, not silvery white like the Chinese. *Vestis sērica* was a more general term, referring doubtless to the Chinese product,[1] which, however, was more often imported raw or in loose fabrics, which were subsequently unravelled and mixed with linen or wool, then rewoven into light and supple stuffs for the so-called *vestēs subsēricae.* By the fourth century of our era these mixed fabrics had come into rather general use; but *vestēs holosēricae,* or garments of pure silk, were still regarded as a great extravagance, used only by very luxurious persons, on state occasions, or for sumptuous gifts. It was the Emperor Justinian who in 552 imported the first silk-worms into Byzantium, whence their culture spread slowly into Western Europe, although only one out of the dozen or more varieties native in China and Japan, 'the *bombȳx mōri,* or mulberry silk-worm, ever became thoroughly naturalized and profitable there.

**The spinning and weaving** of early times was, for the most part, done at home, and was the special business of the mistress of the house, and the maids whom she directed. The spinner held the distaff (*colus*), wrapped about with carded wool, in her left hand, under her left arm, or fastened in her waist-band, while with the right hand she drew out the fibres, fastened them to a hook at the top of the spindle (*fūsus*), and, twirling them slightly between the thumb and forefinger, imparted to

---

[1] The word *Sēres* meant first silk-merchants, but came afterward to be applied to all Chinamen. So that when Virgil speaks (Georg. II. 121) of the Sēres who gather off the trees the soft, fleecy threads which the native worms have left hanging there, he may have used either a commercial or a geographical expression.

the hanging spindle a rotary motion, which continued of itself to twist the lengthening thread. As soon as the spindle touched the floor, it was lifted, the thread already spun was wound around it, and the process repeated. When the spindle was quite full, the thread was removed and laid in the *calathus*, or spinning-basket.

Colus (Rich).

The most primitive looms of all were vertical, and the weaver worked standing. They were very simple in construction, consisting of two parallel bars, to which the threads of the warp were attached, above and below, while the shuttle containing the thread of the woof was passed in and out between them, and back and forth. In such a loom the web might be woven either upwards or downwards. The term *sŭrsum versum*, regularly applied to the *tunicae rēctae*, which young people of both sexes assumed at maturity, is thought to indicate that they were woven from the bottom up. Later on, horizontal looms were introduced, at which the weaver sat. They were identical in principle with the hand-looms of every age and country, and substantially the same in arrangement; and there is scarce a mountain village in Italy to-day where a *contadina* may not be seen tending a fac-simile of the old Roman machine.

All woollen cloths, and, most of all, the home-made fabrics of the early republican period, had to be finished by the fuller (*fullo*) before they were fit for use. They were soaked in pits (*lacūnae*) constructed for the purpose, treated with chalk and other alkalis, dried, washed, and dried again; beaten and carded until the separate threads were no longer visible; finally, brushed, shorn, and pressed.

**The fullers were early organized into a guild** (*collēgium*), with Minerva for their patroness, and an annual feast upon the fifteenth of March; and their art was applied not only to the preparation of new cloths, but to the cleansing and restoration of old garments. A toga made of new cloth, with a full nap, was called a *pexa vestis;* after it had begun to be threadbare it was said to be *trīta* or *defloccāta;* when it had been whitened and restored by the fuller, it was a *toga interpolāta.*

The time soon came, of course, when homespun goods no longer sufficed for the clothing of Rome, and then large factories (*officīnae*) had to be established for the weaving both of woollen and linen cloths. Meanwhile it is certain that, with one very important exception, the art of the *tinctor*, or dyer, was seldom employed upon the old-fashioned home-made fabrics. The natural tints, already noted, of sundry foreign wools, furnished all the variety of color demanded by the taste of a primitive time, especially after it became customary to import colored flocks, which were kept strictly separate from the white home-breeds.

The one exception refers, of course, to that historic purple, which was so highly prized as a mark of social and official rank; whose use at Rome the elder Pliny believes [1] to have been coeval with the city itself, and

[1] Plin. Nat. Hist. ix. 39.

borrowed by her early kings from the conquered sover-
eigns of Etruria.   This famous dye, in all its infinitely
varying shades, was obtained from two kinds of shell-
fish, common in almost every part of the Mediterranean
Sea, — the trumpet shell (*būcinum* or *mūrex*) and the true
purple-shell [1] (*purpura* or *pelagia*).

The juice of the first was crimson, that of the second
nearly black.  It was collected, mixed with salt, and
heated in metal vessels by the introduction of warm
vapor.  The color of the *būcinum* was brilliant, but not
lasting.  By mixing with the darker *purpura* it became
fixed, and those violet or amethystine tints were produced
which appear to have been preferred for the *clāvus lātus*
and the striped borders of white garments.  The true
Tyrian purple, first introduced into Rome about the middle of the last century B.C., was produced by a double
process of dyeing, first in half-boiled *purpura,* and then in
*būcinum*.  A fabric thus dyed appeared nearly black in
shadow, but the high lights upon its folds were of a
glowing red.

A pound of amethyst or violet wool in Cæsar's time
was worth about $20; a pound of real Tyrian, more than
ten times as much.  At a later period, the *blatta* came
into use for both grades of purple, and paler shades than
those of the original dye, as well as a whole range of
blues, were produced by mixing it with different animal
and vegetable substances.  Clear scarlet was obtained
from the *coccus īlicis*, a species of cochineal, and from
the red *fūcus,* or rock-lichen.  The *trabea*, or robe worn
by augurs, and on certain occasions by *equitēs* (knights),

[1] The latter is the *buccinium lapillis*, the former the *murex bran-
daris* of modern conchology.

was of striped scarlet and purple. The *palūdāmentum*,
or short military cloak worn by a Roman general
over his armor, was of a reddish purple, but robes
made entirely of *blatta*, or fine pure purple,
were considered strictly appropriate only
for *triumphātōrēs*, who also had them richly
embroidered, and later for imperial personages. That their use was constantly
affected by others is, however, evinced by
the prohibitive decrees of different emperors, as well as by a very curious passage in Ovid [1] in which he gives it as his
opinion that costly robes of pure purple
are unbecoming to a woman. He advises
instead pale sky-blue or rose pink, a very
faint amethyst, or sea-green. Otherwise the deep tint of
the Paphian myrtle, the soft gray of a crane's plumage,
the brown of acorns or of almond-shells. All this proves
very good taste on the poet's part, and that the superiority in costume of half-tints over pure colors was already
acknowledged by the truly æsthetic.

Paludamentum
(Rich).

**We come now to the form of garments both masculine
and feminine.** From the earliest historic period the
Romans appear to have worn at least two articles of
clothing, — a tunic and a toga. Some wore instead of the
*tunica* an under-garment called the *subligāculum*, which
was little more than such a bandage as the gymnasts
wore when exercising, and which was preferably, if not
always, made of linen. The tunic was necessary indoors,
however, where it was considered bad manners not to
lay the toga aside. The tunic was a species of woollen

[1] Ov. Ars Am. iii. 169–188.

shirt, made with front and back pieces, which were sewn together on the shoulders and under the arms. Either it had no sleeves, or the sleeves were short, not reaching below the elbow. Long-sleeved tunics (*tunicae manicātae* or *manuleātae*) were considered the height of effeminacy, and never came into general use before the third or fourth century of our era. The tunics of the common people were belted in above the hips, and did not hang below the knee. Those who were entitled to the *clāvus lātus*, or broad purple stripe down the front, which was always so arranged as to hang outside the girdle, wore them somewhat longer; soldiers and travellers, even shorter. In the time of Plautus it had become customary to wear also an undershirt or tunic, called the *tunica interior* or *subūcula*, which was also regularly made of wool, never of linen, until late imperial times.

Tunica (Rich).

**We have already seen how the toga** was first put on at the age of maturity, with public and impressive ceremonies. It remains to say a few words concerning the shape and arrangement of this celebrated garment. It was of white woollen cloth, which in the case of curule magistrates had narrow purple stripes inwoven for a border. It appears to have come from the loom in an oblong form, and afterwards to have been rounded at the corners into that of an ellipse. Its length must be three times the wearer's height measured downwards from the shoulder. Its breadth varied greatly with time, fashion, and the quality of the cloth. The toga of the early period was comparatively narrow, and the rough, coarse fabric of which it was made permitted no artistic arrangement. In those days the toga was the garment of war as well as of peace, and when worn in the field it had no loosely hanging ends, but was bound tightly around the body in what was called the *cinctus Gabīnus.* Later, after the introduction of the *sagum*, or short square military cloak, fastened upon the shoulder with a *fībula*, or brooch, the toga became the distinctive garb of peace, and gave scope for enormous vanity, both in its texture and in the mode of wearing it. It was made of ever finer and finer cloth, the supple folds of which were assiduously studied and arranged. The broader the cloth, it was observed, the more graceful the effect which could be given these folds, hence the fashionable toga increased in width, until it became nearly circular, and Horace jeers[1] at the freedman who paraded the Sacred Way in a toga four yards (*bis trium ūlnārum*) wide, to the scandal of the passers-by.

Cinctus Gabinus (Rich).

This elliptical garment was first folded, not exactly on its longest axis, but so as to leave the edges a little way apart. One end of the folded cloth was now flung over the left shoulder from behind so as to fall to the feet in front. The remaining two-thirds of its length were then brought around under the right arm, and the folded cloth so spread as to cover the right side from the armpit to the calf of the leg. It was then gathered and carried up

[1] Hor. Epod. iv. 7, 8.

across the breast, to be thrown backward over the left shoulder. The diagonal breast-folds constituted the *sinus*, which often served the purposes of a pocket. The portion of the toga first thrown over the left shoulder, and lying beneath the *sinus*, was in later times pulled up so as to hang a little way over it in what was called the *nōdus*, or *umbō*. This precaution was supposed to give firmness to the whole arrangement; but the toga must always, one would think, have been fastened to the tunic, at least upon the shoulder, else it is impossible to conceive how the wearer could have had any freedom either of locomotion or gesticulation. There seems some reason to believe that the toga of imperial times was cut out in the form of a semi-ellipse, and partially fitted to the person, while a portion was pressed into fine folds by the fuller before wearing. At the opening of the temple of Janus at the Ambarvalia, or ceremony of blessing the fields for a good harvest (which was observed on May 27th, and is still observed in most Latin countries), and upon certain other solemn public occasions, the Gabinian or girded toga was regularly worn.

Candidates for office derived their name from the custom which required them to appear in a *toga candida*, or pure white toga, either quite new or freshly treated with chalk. The mourning toga was originally black; later the darkest blue was also worn.

The working-classes used, for defence against the weather, an outer cloak called *paenula*, made of thick, hairy, dark-colored frieze, or even of leather. It had no sleeves, but was usually provided with a hood (*cucŭllus*), and hooked or buttoned closely all down the front. The obvious convenience and snugness of this garment caused it eventually to be adopted as a travelling wrap by men, and even women, of all ranks, and the host's first duty to a guest was to unfasten his *paenula*.[1]

The *birrus* or *burrus* was another outside garment of similar cut, made usually of rough, red cloth. The *lacerna* was of lighter and more elegant material, and worn outside the toga, less for use than for show. Evening-dress, as we understand it, was represented by the *vestis cēnātōria*, which appears to have been an exceedingly light and airy mantle, presumably of rich material, and almost always gaily colored, — green, blue, crimson, and variegated. It was easily thrown on and off and sometimes changed several times in the course of one ceremonious dinner.

**The primitive Roman, like the barbarian everywhere, was long-haired and long-bearded.** The razor and the shears — *novācula* and *forfex* — are indeed mentioned early, the former in the reign of Tarquinius Priscus; but we are expressly told by the elder Pliny,[2] that Scipio Africanus was the first Roman who ever shaved daily, while the beard of Augustus was always cut. The first hair cut from the head of a child, and a youth's first beard, were consecrated to the gods; but the coins of the late republican period show plainly that young men usually wore a beard, though carefully trimmed and dressed, and were seldom clean-shaven before forty. To

---

[1] Hence, too, *scindere paenulam* (to rend the cloak) became proverbial for giving a visitor a pressing invitation to remain; and we find Cicero saying to Atticus (Ep. xiii. 33) of an unwelcome guest, "*Sed ita feci, ut non scinderem paenulam,*" meaning that he sent him about his business without delay.

[2] Plin. Nat. Hist. vii. 59.

let the beard grow long was a sign of mourning, whether for private loss or public calamity, and continued to be so regarded until the Emperor Hadrian re-introduced the fashion of the full beard even for middle-aged and elderly men.

There were frequent changes, also, in the mode of masculine hair-dressing. In Cicero's time it was elaborate, and depilatories and hair-tongs (*psīlōthra* and *calamistrī*) were among the barber's regular weapons, whether the latter were a house-slave, or the keeper of a *tōnstrīna*, or barber's shop. In the time of Marcus Aurelius the artificially curled and perfumed head was no longer considered in good taste. Later, it became fashionable for even imperial personages to wear the hair close-clipped, like athletes and the Stoics.

**For head-gear** the Romans had the *pīleus* and the *petasus.* The former was a close-fitting felt cap, worn by

Pileus (Rich).

sailors and artisans, by a freedman as the sign of his emancipation, and by the whole population on the Saturnalia, but otherwise used by the upper classes only when journeying. The *petasus* was a felt hat with a round brim, worn principally by comic actors, and by the spectators in a theatre, as a protection against the light from above. A well-born Roman of the best period, however, — whether man or woman, —

Petasus (Rich).

usually disdained any species of hat or cap, but walked abroad uncovered.

**For the clothing of their feet,** the Romans made use both of shoes (*calceī*) and sandals (*sandalia*). Every Roman order and every great tribe or *gēns* had a distinctive kind of shoe. The ordinary *calceus patricius,* or patrician shoe, also called *mūlleus,* was made of red leather, with a high heel, and straps to fasten it about the ankle. It had also a crescent-shaped ornament upon the front, called the *lūnula,* which was of very ancient origin, and seems, like the *bulla,* to have had the force of a charm. The second grade of

Shoes and sandals (Becker's Gallus).

shoe, only a little less dignified than the *mūlleus,* was the *calceus senātōrius,* which was of black leather, with four straps and no *lūnula.* Another kind of shoe, called the *pēro,* and rather resembling a boot, worn in wet or snowy weather, and always by the *equitēs,* was also black, and fastened by a simple tie. The ladies of the higher classes wore, out of doors, *calceī,* made of a fine leather called *alūta,* and richly embroidered in silk and gold. At home, both men and women preferred to wear sandals, or simple soles, bound to the foot with straps or ribbons, but it was long regarded as a great breach of etiquette to wear sandals abroad. The craft of the *sūtor,* or shoe-maker, was always a particularly respectable one, and theirs was one of the original colleges founded by Numa.

**The civilized Roman lady, like her lord of the same period, wore three garments, —** a *tunica intima*, a *stola*, and a *palla*. The woollen undergarment was virtually the same for both sexes. The *stola* was much longer than the masculine tunic, slit open at the top on either side for the passage of the arms, fastened again upon the shoulders with clasps or brooches (*fībulae*), which were often articles of great value. It was usually finished at the bottom by a ruffled border or flounce called the *instita*, which admitted of embroidery or other decoration. Sometimes it had tight sleeves reaching to the elbow and fastened together on the back of the arm with gold or jewelled buttons, a charming mode, represented upon many existing statues. The *stola* was confined at the waist by a girdle, but pulled up so as to conceal the latter by its falling folds (*rūgae*). This beautiful garment was the matron's robe of honor, and only married women of unblemished reputation were allowed to wear it.

Euterpe with stola and palla
(Baumeister).

The *palla* was the outer garment which took the place of the *toga,* and was worn in a similar way. It was a square or oblong piece of stuff, thrown forward over the left shoulder and falling to the feet, then carried around the back, either above or below the right arm, and again thrown backward over the left arm or shoulder. Like the *toga,* it could, if necessary, be drawn up over the head. Women of the lower orders, or those not privileged to wear the *stola* wore, directly over the under-tunic, a *palla* made of woollen cloth, turned over at the top and folded round the body under the arms, then drawn up and fastened upon either shoulder with clasps or simple buckles. It thus lay double over the breast and back, but fell in a single thickness to the feet. To judge by the management of the folds in existing illustrations, the stuffs most affected for their outer garments by Roman women who aspired to elegance, were always fine and thin. The mixed fabrics already described, of silk and wool or silk and linen, were probably most employed, pure silk being always an article of great luxury, while the very fine linen and cotton stuffs to which the word *byssus* was indifferently applied, were a late fashion and fit only for summer garments.

We have already learned from Ovid how wide was the range of colors from which a Roman belle could choose. She enjoyed hardly less latitude in her hair-dressing, the styles of which were infinite. The graceful antique fashion had been to gather the hair altogether in a knot at the back of the head, sometimes low in the neck, but oftener lifted high upon the crown, and we find the early fathers of the Christian Church, — Jerome, Tertullian, Prudentius, — pleading earnestly for a return to this

decent and simple mode, and sternly denouncing the
ugly and costly artificial structure of cushions, braids,
and curls then greatly in vogue. Entire wigs (*capillā-
menta*) were much worn in the first century, and those
made of blonde hair brought very high prices.

**Gold and jewelled ornaments,** *annuli* (rings), *monīlia*
(necklaces), *armillae* (bracelets), worn either at the wrist
or above the elbow, with a sleeveless tunic, were affected
both by men and women of fashion, and were often of
exquisite workmanship. All the principal precious stones,
diamonds, rubies, emeralds, opals, were known to the
Romans, but the gem which they prized above all others
was the pearl; and unheard-of prices were paid for large
single specimens, to be worn as ear-drops or upon the
brow. Julius Cæsar is said to have given to Servilia, the
mother of Marcus Brutus,[1] a solitaire pearl for which he
paid six million sesterces ($262,500), while Caligula
received with his wife Lollia Paulina a complete *parure*
of pearls and emeralds, which was an heirloom in her
family; a part of the spoil taken in Eastern war by her
grandfather, Marcus Lollius, in the year 2 B.C., and valued at forty million sesterces [2] ($2,180,000). Slippers
embroidered with seed pearls were common among the
rich, and sometimes affected, as the elder Pliny complains,
even by the comparatively poor.

[1] Suet. Caes. 50.          [2] Plin. Nat. Hist. ix. 35.

# CHAPTER V.

## AGRICULTURE.

SMALL holdings were certainly the rule among the early Romans. Tradition even averred that Romulus had allotted to each of his followers but two *iūgera*[1] of land. After the expulsion of the kings, the tribune Licinius was said to have decreed an allowance per capita of seven *iūgera*. This did not apparently prevent a proprietor from increasing his possessions if he saw fit, but laws more decidedly restrictive had soon to be passed. Five hundred *iūgera* was fixed as the maximum holding, and one of the reforms which the Gracchi favored was a further reduction to two hundred.

The former number remained the nominal maximum down to historic times, and even after the restrictive law had become a dead letter, there was a sentiment in favor of small holdings. "Praise large farms, but till a small one," is the witty precept of Virgil.[2]

Naturally, as the farm increased in extent, the mode of working it became more complex. Two *iūgera* the owner could manage without assistance; when his possessions increased to seven, he may have had a slave or two to aid him, and perhaps an ass; but seven *iūgera* would certainly not support a pair of oxen, and indeed

---

[1] About 1¼ acres: see table.     [2] Geor. ii. 412–18.

the spade always held its own against the plough in Roman agriculture.

In the management of large holdings three methods appear to have been practised. A farm might be let for a fixed money rent, or let on shares with the rent paid in kind, or the owner might choose to be his own farmer, making use of either slave labor or free, or what was perhaps most common of all, having a permanent staff of slaves, and supplementing these with hired hands at the seasons when work pressed, as at the vintage.

**In choosing a farmstead,** the chief thing to be avoided was an unhealthy district. A marshy soil was always to be shunned, and so was a river-bank, though an ample water-supply was indispensable. The ideal situation was a hillside gently sloping to the east. Here the master's residence could be adapted to receive the sun in winter and the breeze in summer, drainage was easily managed, and the very best soil for vineyards and olive-orchards secured. Facility of transportation for the farm-produce was a great desideratum, yet Columella[1] advises against a situation immediately on a high-road, both on account of the depredations of the casual passer-by, and because of the perpetual calls on the owner's hospitality.

The estate purchased, the proprietor's first care was to have its boundaries clearly established. There was a pleasant fashion of following its outer line with a close-set row of trees all of one kind, as elm, ash, or cypress; or it might be enclosed with hedge or fence, or by a ditch and earthen bank. Otherwise its limits were indicated merely by boundary stakes.

The next point to be considered was the choice of a

[1] Col. De Re Rus. i. 5.

crop adapted to the soil, and we find great difference of opinion among the writers on agriculture as to those which promised the best return. All agree, however, in lamenting that so many estates were given over to the grazing of cattle and sheep, to the detriment of agriculture proper. The majority follow Cato in giving their first preference to a choice vineyard, though the vine required more labor than any other crop. To one hundred *iūgera* of vineyard Cato allows ten laborers, one ox-herd, and one yoke of oxen, one ass-driver with three asses (two for the carts and one for the mill), a swine-herd, and a man to look after the willow plantations, from which came the withies for binding the vine, while all the osier baskets required in stripping the vines, gathering the grapes, etc., were woven on the premises.

Two hundred and forty *iūgera* of olive-orchards were stated by the same authority to require five laborers, three ox-herds for as many yoke of oxen, a pig-tender, an ass-driver with four asses, and a shepherd with a hundred sheep.

**The farm-hands,** whether many or few, were always under the supervision of a *vīlicus* and *vīlica*, an overseer and a housekeeper, as we might say.[1] This pair was often, though not invariably, husband and wife. The overseer had to keep a sharp lookout over the slaves by night and day, provide their food and clothing, see that the farm-tools were in good condition, and in general that everything might be ready for the master's inspection at any moment. The sphere of the *vīlica* was within doors, except for the care of the *gallīnārium*,

---

[1] These offices are perpetuated on the Italian villa farm, where a *fattore* and *fattoressa* are always to be found.

or poultry-yard, where, if there were ever a dearth of
fowls or eggs, she was the person held responsible.
She saw to the cooking and sweeping, the pickling
and preserving. She was also warned to be no gad-
about, and not to presume to offer any sacrifices; for
the master of the house undertook the religious respon-
sibilities of the whole *familia*. Yet on feast-days, and
on the Calends, Nones, and Ides of each month, she
was to adorn her hearth with a wreath of flowers, and
offer to the *Larēs* her prayers for plenty.

**The food of the familia rūstica** consisted of a liberal
daily allowance of bread, wine, oil, salt, and some sort
of relish, such as pickled olives or fish. Every two years
the hands received a pair of wooden shoes, and on alternate years a tunic and a hooded cloak of shaggy cloth
(*sagātus cucūllus*). They were also supplied with patch-
work coverings called *centōnēs*, made up by the female
slaves from the sound bits of all sorts of cast-off garments, which might be used either as bedding, or by way
of protection from the rain. Special favors in the
matter of diet and clothing were often shown to highly
deserving slaves; but the punishment, even of trifling
offences, was frequently barbarous.

The slaves were divided into those who worked in
fetters (*compeditī, alligatī*), and those who were allowed
liberty of motion; and a great distinction was made in
their housing; for while the latter had a large common
room where they might meet in the evening and on
rainy days, and separate cells to sleep in, airy, above
ground, and with a southern aspect, the former were
lodged in basements lighted only by narrow windows too
high to be reached by the hand, and in these underground

chambers refractory cases were kept at indoor work by day. There would also be upon large properties a separate *balneum*, or bath, for the slaves.

The farmer is earnestly warned against over-building; but the constructions prescribed as necessary for the farm activities seem to furnish an ample allowance. The rapid increase of luxury in the two hundred and fifty years between Cato and Columella is clearly shown by the difference in their provisions. The buildings enumerated by the latter are certainly more elaborate than anything to be found upon Italian farms to-day, though many of his precepts are still implicitly obeyed. And since he, too, prefaces his description by strenuous injunctions not to build too extensively, his account may be taken as affording a fair idea of an affluent Roman farmstead.

**The master's dwelling,** or villa proper, stood a little apart from the rest of the buildings, with long ranges of rooms for summer and winter, covered galleries, and a separate bath. Nearly all the other structures were grouped about a great central court-yard (*cors*), which was carefully enclosed, and had but a single gateway, affording the only means of entrance not merely to the court-yard itself, but to the surrounding stables and store-houses. Over this gateway in large establishments a porter or janitor always presided. In those of less pretension, the *vīlicus* had his rooms there, and it was his place to see that no one passed after dark without his knowledge. Here, too, was chained the watch-dog, with the broad spiked collar, familiar to us from old mosaics, who had been carefully trained to his duties of defence. On this same side of the court-yard were the slaves' quarters and the farm-kitchen.

The court-yard was always kept strewn with litter, which was removed from time to time, and added to the manure-heaps. These last were built within the court, and allowed to ripen for at least a twelvemonth, before being applied to the land. Here, too, was a pool of fresh water, not only for watering the stock, but large enough for oxen to bathe in. It was supplied by running water, where this was practicable, in other cases, by rain-water, which the Romans well understood the art of collecting and utilizing.

First in importance among the *stabula*, or buildings for sheltering the animals, were the *būbīlia* for the oxen and cows. These were long, narrow buildings, usually set at right angles with one side of the court-yard, and they accommodated only a single range of cattle, with room for a passage-way before their mangers. Six or seven feet above the ground ran a horizontal beam, to which the animals were tied. The flooring was of wood or stone, and well bedded with coarse hay or straw, and the barn seems often, if not always, to have had a loft for storing fodder.

**Cattle were bred** rather with a view to their powers of draught, than for beef, as is clearly seen in the points given of a model ox. The favorite color was red or dun, though we find frequent allusions to the fine silver gray breed of Central Italy, still extensively maintained. On account of the difficulty of acclimatizing foreign breeds, the farmer who wished to form a herd was advised to buy young cattle in his own neighborhood, and to make the following stipulation with the vendor:[1] "Do you answer for it, that these two-year-olds are perfectly

[1] Varr. R. R. ii. 5.

sound, and from a healthy herd, and that the purchase of them will involve me in no trouble ?"

Bullocks were usually broken to the plough when three years old, and this was most carefully and thoroughly done, as was indeed necessary, seeing that the man who held the plough drove as well. This slave, the *bŭbulcus*, also took care of his yoke of oxen, washing and carding them, and giving them a sort of *massage* treatment, supposed to prevent the skin from adhering to the flesh. He is further recommended to give them each a quart of wine if they come back tired from the field.[1]

The working of from eighty to a hundred *iŭgera* was given to one yoke of oxen; but in ploughing, they were only allowed to draw, without breathing, what seems to us the incredibly short furrow of one hundred and twenty Roman feet.[2] The yoke (*iŭgum*) was sometimes fastened to the horns in the present Italian fashion, by which all the draught comes upon the forehead; but more often rested, as with us, upon the neck; but in place of a closed wooden bow, leathern thongs (*lora*) were tied around the neck. Neither oxen nor horses were shod, as we understand the term, but they often wore a sort of leathern boot (*solea*), which was strengthened upon its sole by strips of metal. This fashion seems to have been later than Cato, who recommends protecting their hoofs against cracking, on long journeys over the paved high-roads, by daubing them with pitch.

In many parts of Italy the climate was genial enough to afford fresh fodder all the year round; in which case

[1] In England, hunters are often given beer after a hard run.
[2] See Tables.

a farmer was advised to double the number of his yokes
of oxen and work and pasture on alternate days. When
stable-fed, the oxen received hay, straw, barley, and other
grain. But besides these staple articles, many others
figure in their diet, such as beans and acorns, the refuse
of the vintage, and the freshly plucked leaves of many
trees.

A hundred was considered the extreme limit in number of a herd of cows, and these were chiefly kept for
breeding; for it must be remembered that butter was
unknown to the Romans, though cheese was a common
article of food.

Very singular and sometimes very unpleasant remedies
are recommended by the Roman authorities for the
various diseases to which neat flesh is liable. The
following is declared by Cato [1] to be an almost universal
panacea: "a raw egg swallowed whole, to be followed
next morning by an onion bruised in a half-pint of wine.
Let a fasting man see that the ox drinks this fasting,

Equile, stable (Rich).

and let both man and
beast stand while it is
being swallowed."

The *būbīlia* were re-
quired to have a south-
ern exposure for warmth
in winter, and a shady
yard adjoining, where
the cattle might be
turned out in summer.

Many of the same general prescriptions held good for the
*equīlia*, or stables for horses and mules; but these were

[1] De Re Rus. lxxi.

also provided with separate cribs fitted with racks, and though single stalls seem to have been unknown, it was customary to divide the horses by a swinging pole called the *longurius*, which prevented their interfering with one another. The breeds of horses were innumerable, some being preferred for one purpose and some for another.

**Race-horses** commanded the highest prices, choice mules the next, then ordinary animals, whether intended for carriage, saddle, or draught. These last might be broken in at two years old; but the race-horses waited another year, and nearly as much more time was spent in their training, so that they were four when they went upon the track. Horses were carefully cleaned and rubbed down each day; but it seems to have been thought necessary to give them bedding only if their stable had a stone floor. Columella says, however,[1] that oak-wood is much better.

The high feeding of horses is insisted upon; also broad meadow-lands, where the grass is short and sweet, and the water-supply unfailing, are recommended for their pasturage. The Romans, like ourselves, judged of a horse's age chiefly by his teeth, and their knowledge of his anatomy was surprisingly accurate; but the medicaments with which he was treated when out of condition show a very elementary stage of equine pathology.

**Asses were much used upon a Roman farm;** for, besides serving as beasts of burden, —and, if fitted with a pair of paniers, they can carry a surprisingly heavy load, — they were also used for light ploughing, to turn the mill, and to raise water from the wells. Black or spotted

[1] Re Rus. vi. 30.

asses were preferred to mouse-colored, merely because
they were more rarely found.

**Nothing could be more generally useful upon a Roman
farm than a flock of sheep.** Lamb and mutton, it is
true, appeared only upon the tables of the rich, but the
milk of ewes, and the cheese made from it, were important articles of diet, and their fleece furnished the
clothing of the family. White was the color preferred,
though certain breeds of black and brown found some
favor, and fancy breeds of various colors, notably a
reddish yellow, from Baetica in Spain, were raised as
curiosities. Sheep were also broadly divided into two
classes, soft and harsh fleeced, of which the former were
more delicate, and their wool more valuable. Out of
many breeds, the farmer is recommended to choose that
which may best suit the pasturage at his disposal,
and to be careful that the stock is pure, for the one
perfectly worthless fleece was grizzled or spotted. So,
in a white flock, lambs were to be rejected, not only if
they had any spots of dark color on fleece or skin, but if
their tongue and palate were black — an infallible sign
of mixed breed.

Sheep were turned out to pasture during some part of
the day, nearly all the year round, the morning and
evening frost being avoided in winter, and the mid-day
heat in summer. For the same reason, though the
sheep-fold (*ovile*) was built low and narrow to protect
the flock in winter, it had always a large and shady
yard adjoining, where they could be turned out in summer. The fine-wooled sheep, as those of Tarentum, were
chiefly fed indoors, while the reverse was true of the
coarser breeds; but the shepherd is warned that his

wards must never under any circumstances go hungry, and also that they will soon weary of any kind of food and fall seriously ill unless they have an abundance of salt. If the sheep were to browse, the pasturage must be free from those thorny brambles which were so injurious both to the fleece of the animal and to its skin when freshly sheared. The shepherd is also to keep a sharp lookout for snakes. Virgil recommends smoking them out of their holes by fires of cedar and other aromatic woods, but Columella considers it a more efficient precaution frequently to burn women's hair or stag's horn in and about the fold.

**The Romans sheared their sheep,** as we do, in the spring; but they preferred that lambing-time should come in the autumn, winter being considered a less dangerous season than summer for young flocks. A thousand head of sheep might be folded together with safety, but a shepherd was allotted to every hundred, and each shepherd seems to have been accompanied by a dog. These dogs were apparently the direct ancestors of those who guard the flocks upon the Roman Campagna to-day, and no one who has made the acquaintance of the latter can read without a grim smile the following suggestion of Columella:[1] "The shepherd prefers to have his dog white, as this color contrasts with that of wild beasts. And it is important to have some such broad distinction, or else when he is driving off the wolves in the dim light of dawn, he is likely to hit the dog instead of the beast." It may be noticed that docking a dog's tail was supposed to be a preventive of hydrophobia.

The shepherds and goat-herds also set up temporary

[1] Re Rus. vii. 12.

huts of conical shape (*casulae*) for shelter, as their successors do to-day ; but one object now aimed at, that of raising themselves sufficiently from the surface of the ground to be out of the reach of the malarious fogs which only rise a few feet above the Campagna soil, did not exist when the region was generally and very efficiently drained.

**Next in importance to the sheep came the black-coated, silky goats,** from whose hair ropes were woven, and a fabric cheaper and coarser than cloths manufactured from sheep's wool, but to a certain extent water-proof. They were less delicate, too, than sheep and could be pastured on rougher ground, and it was probably for this reason that a goat-herd had charge of only half as many animals as a shepherd. He was to be a sturdy man, with a quick eye and a sure foot, for his flock had to be led, not driven, by him, as was the case with most other creatures. Cheese was made from the milk of goats as well as from that of ewes and cows, and there were several varieties, from the simple curd for immediate use, to one which would keep indefinitely and even bear transportation over sea. Cheeses made from ewes' milk were considered more digestible though less palatable than those made from cows' milk, while the reverse was supposed to be the case with goats'-milk cheeses.

**Black-haired pigs** were insisted upon for cold districts; but if the climate were mild, the more tender white breeds might be raised. Each sow was given a separate pen opening on a central yard, where there was a tank of water, but this opening had a barrier so high that while the sow could get over it, her pigs could not. They were driven to woodland pasture nearly all the year, and even when kept in, acorns were still the chief article of their diet, though beans were also given them. They were thought fit for sacrifice when ten days old (whence *sacer* was the name of a ten-days-old pig among the early Romans); and if there were a market-town near by, it was considered most profitable to sell them as sucking pigs. Hogs were also fattened for the sale, and Varro mentions with admiration that they were sometimes made too fat to stand upon their feet.

So far, the arrangements of the farm show merely a legitimate development from the early Roman methods; but when we come to its feathered denizens, we perceive at once the overweening influence of Greek fashion. Greek names, in their original form, or barely Latinized, are continually employed, while the Romans quite vaunt themselves on having stood out against the Grecian practice of cock-fighting. The game-cock was, however, the favorite breed in Italy as well as in Greece. **Two hundred hens were considered a fair number for a flock,** and one man, with a child's help, could take care of so many. The following was the most approved way of housing them. The central hen-coop (*gallīnārium*), seven Roman feet on each of its three dimensions, was flanked on either side by a wing of the same breadth, twelve feet high and twelve feet long, divided into two stories by a flooring seven feet from the ground. These wings had no outer door, but communicated through the central coop, which opened on the court-yard, where the fowls were turned out, to scratch and feed through the day. The walls were pierced with windows, which were, however, securely barred against the incursions of evil beasts. Two fashions of providing the hens with nests obtained: the first was to hang osier baskets along the walls; the other, and more approved method, was to build these walls so thick that rows of nests could be hollowed out of them, like the niches in a columbarium. In either case, a *vēstibulum*, or perch, was provided before each nest, so that the hens might not break their eggs by flying straight upon them. Notched stakes served them for stairways to the upper stories of the wings, and the whole coop, like all *aviāria*, was to be coated within and without with highly polished cement, as a precaution against cats and snakes.

Cleanliness was greatly insisted on, as well here as in the more elaborate geese and duck yards (*chēnoboscīa* and *nessotrophīa*). Hens were fed upon various kinds of dough, and their water-dishes were fitted with covers pierced with holes large enough to allow the head to pass easily through, whereby, also, the water was kept clean.

**The dove-cote** (*columbārium*) was arranged on the same general principles, except that it was constructed high above the ground, and the purchase of white pigeons as well as that of white hens was discouraged because of their being conspicuous objects to birds of prey. Pigeons certainly commanded fancy prices, *ducēnī nummī* (about nine dollars) being thought a fair amount for a pair of perfect birds even in Varro's time, while five times this amount was not uncommon.

**Thrushes** (*turdī*) were caught and fattened for the markets, as were also blackbirds (*merulae*), ortolans (*mīliāriae*), quails (*cōturnīcēs*), and other wild fowl. This class of winged creature was all housed together, often to the number of several thousand. The *ornīthon*, as their place of confinement was called, was often built along a covered walk, and separated from it only by a netting, so that the owner might admire his treasures as he took his daily exercise; but this is not recommended by all authorities, some being of opinion that the spirits of free-born birds were depressed in captivity by the sight of vegetation.

**Peacocks** also (*pāvōnēs*) were kept for show from early times, but after Quintus Hortensius had set the fashion of eating them, their cultivation became one of the most profitable industries of the Roman farmer; for their eggs fetched ten dollars a dozen, and the birds themselves seventeen dollars a pair. Their coops and feeding-ground were usually, however, at a considerable distance from the farm-yard.

This was also the case with water-fowl, for whose well-being the most elaborate arrangements were made. They had great yards set apart for them, surrounded by high and smoothly polished walls, and covered by a strong netting. In the yard was a pond, fed by running water, supplied with gently sloping verges, and planted with all the most palatable water-weeds, while around its grassy brim, nests were built, separated from each other by box-hedges and furnished with troughs for the daily supply of grain.

In the luxurious days of Rome, fish and wild animals were preserved even on comparatively modest estates, and a snail-yard was rarely absent.

**Bee-culture** received great attention from the Romans, in whose diet honey took the place of sugar. The superlative excellence of pot-herbs, and above all thyme, for flavoring honey, was insisted on by all writers, but no one has described this branch of agriculture so charmingly as Virgil.

To return to the court-yard and the buildings about it. There were sheds for the housing of unthreshed grain and unpressed olives, granaries and storerooms for fruit, wine, and oil. Fodder was more often stacked than housed, but farm-implements were kept under cover, and the more portable of them under lock and key. In small tools the farmer of those days was perhaps deficient, but for working the land his means were abundant. The long prevalence of hand labor probably accounted for the astonishing variety of spades, mattocks, and rakes,

for whose Latin names it is not always easy to find exact English equivalents. The *rutrum*, the weapon with which Remus was killed, was a kind of shovel. They had a sort of spade called the *pāla*, both with iron and wooden blade, and this implement was sometimes made with a

Rutrum (Rich).

cross-bar for the foot to rest on. The latter tool is called in Italian *vanga*, a name which is also found in late Latin. For digging, spading over the land, breaking up fresh soil, etc., the Romans used tools of the nature of the mattock, which, while they did the work of a spade, were handled like a hoe. Under this head came the *ligo* (also used as a hatchet); the *bidēns*, with blade notched into two teeth; the *capreolus*, where these two teeth were curved inward like a goat's horns, and the *rāster*,

Bidens (Rich).

which looks like a horseshoe tied to a handle. These were all heavy enough to do the work of the plough, and were indeed thought to break up the ground more efficiently.

The names of *ditcher* and *ditching* ( *fossor* and *fossio*), given to the man who thus dug over the ground and to the work which he performed, shows that the earth must have been thrown in successive cuts from one side to the other of a perpetual trench, and there was a clever little machine, the *cicōnia*, for testing the faithfulness of the labor and making sure that this trench was kept straight and of unvarying depth and width.

Of lighter weight than the tools already mentioned were the *marra*, with broad, notched blade, and the *sarculum* and *āscia*, which nearly corresponded to a long and short handled hoe. The *rāster* was also found with several teeth, and its diminutive, *rāstellum*, was a wooden rake; the *pecten* was yet another rake, perhaps of iron.

*Falx* is the general name for scythe, sickle, hedge-bill, or other agricultural implement of like nature. Most curious of all was the *falx vīnitōria*, the vine-dresser's pruning-hook, with

Falx vinitoria (Rich).

its many edges. Columella[1] gives a minute description of this tool, which would very well describe the more elaborate of English hedge-bills. The *falx denticulāta* must also be noted, a sickle with saw-toothed

Falx denticula (Rich). blade, for cutting the grain just below the ear, a practice recommended as facilitating its threshing. The Romans had both a two-pronged iron fork (*furca*) and a wooden one with many teeth, used

[1] De Re Rus. iv. 25.

for tossing the straw lightly about the threshing-floor, that the wind might detach the chaff, and hence called *ventilābrum*.

Leaving the hand-tools we pass to those which had to be worked by cattle. Of these, the most important was, of course, the *arātrum*, or plough. In its primitive form

Arator (Rich).

it was made entirely of wood. A stout-branched sapling was chosen, with a sharp curve, one end was pointed for the *vōmer*, or share, while the other end was left long enough to serve as a pole (*tēmo*) for the oxen; at the point of junction (*būris*) between *tēmo* and *vōmer*, a handle (*stīva*) was inserted, which the ploughman (*arātor*) held in guiding. A plough hardly more elaborate than the one here described is still used

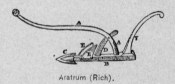

Aratrum (Rich).

in the wilder and remoter parts of Italy. Virgil's plough [1] is certainly a slight advance on this, and in later Imperial times the Romans had ploughs with nearly every feature of our own, though ruder in construction. They had ploughs with coulters and without, ploughs both with and without wheels, ploughs with no mould-board, with one, and with two, some with broad shares, and some with narrow, to suit the nature of the soil, and their two-fold service of

[1] Virg. Geor. i. 169–175.

breaking ground and ploughing in seed. It appears clear, however, that the plough in common use could not turn over a furrow when held in an upright position, but must be guided a little obliquely, that the weight of the beam might bear on the freshly cut earth. This process made a sloping narrow furrow, and in order thoroughly to work the ground, good farmers commonly turned back (as the double face of their share permitted) and ploughed a full, upright furrow in the same line. The necessity for going twice over the ground made the advantages of the *arātrum* over the *bidēns* much less than those of the plough over the spade. A bas-relief found in the island of Magnesia shows one of the ploughs which were adapted for covering in the seed, and making a channel for water between the ridges, an instrument which was in constant use in the palmy days of agriculture about Rome. The plough here depicted has for share-beam (*dentāle*) a narrow plank some four feet long, shod at its forward end with an iron share (*vōmer*), which extends above and below the beam, like an arrow-head on its staff. To the sides of the *dentāle*, directly behind the share, are fastened the double mould-boards (*aurēs*), which turned up a ridge on either side of the line drawn by the passage of the plough. Behind the mould-boards comes the curving pole (*tēmo*), supported by a truss, and at the extreme end the single guiding handle (*stīva*).

The Roman *irpex* was a plank set with teeth and drawn by oxen over the ground. Its use was not that of our harrow (the work of which was usually done by hand), but to clear the ground of small roots; so, though this is not expressly stated, its teeth were probably set at an angle. A species of brush-harrow called *crātēs* was, however, employed. The *trĭbulum* was a platform studded with nails, drawn over the grain upon the threshing-floor to open the ears. Unyoked cattle were sometimes driven about over the threshing-floor for the same purpose, and flails (*perticae*) also were used (these were merely long, pliable rods), especially when the grain had been reaped just below the ear, and was, therefore, almost free of straw.

The proper mode of preparing the threshing-floor is described by all the authorities, but nowhere more clearly than by Virgil in the first Georgic.

The rooms containing the oil and wine presses also opened on the central court-yard. To the harvest of two hundred and forty *iŭgera* of olive-orchards, Cato assigns three mills, one worked by a donkey, one by hand, and one so-called Spanish mill; but his estimates are confessedly made with a wide margin for accidents. **These mills,** which all bore the same name (*molae*), as those used for grinding grain, were probably very like the latter in construction. The lower stone (*mēta*) was immovable; the upper (*catĭllus*) turned about it exactly as in the

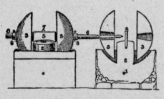

Trapetum (Rich).

former case; and by this means the fleshy part of the berry was detached from the stone and bruised, while the latter was left intact. The *trapētum* was a more elaborate machine for performing the same office, and to these two Columella gives the preference over all other mills. When cleared of stones, the pulp was put under the press (*torcular*), which consisted merely of boards forced down by a press-beam (*prēlum*), working like a long-armed lever. In the time of Pliny, this was replaced by the much more compact and effective screw-press. The juice expressed by the *torcular* was guided by the slope of the floor into one or more earthen jars sunk below its level, and from these the permanent receptacles were filled. The construction and working of the wine-press was very similar, if indeed the same machine were not used for both fruits.

**That the Romans had a great many species of grain** appears from the long catalogue of names furnished by the writers on agriculture, but it is no longer easy to determine the exact nature of all these varieties. Both autumn and spring sowing were practised, as with us, though the former was preferred. About a bushel of wheat (*trīticum*) was used to a *iūgerum*, and this amount of land required four days' ploughing with oxen, one of harrowing, two days for the first hoeing, one for the second, one for weeding, and one and a half for harvesting. In this estimate the sowing is plainly included under the head of ploughing. The ground was ploughed three times; the first broke up the earth, the second cross-ploughed it, the third traced the drills in which the seed was sown by hand and harrowed[1] in. The first hoeing (*sarrītio*) banked up the earth about the young grain and cleared it of weeds; the weeding (*runcātio*) consisted in lopping with a sickle the tops of the weeds, their roots not being disturbed. The cultivation of all grains followed these general lines.

[1] The *occātio* or harrowing was performed either by the *crātēs* or by the *rāstrum*.

**Pulse formed an essential article of food** both for man and beast, and ranked next in importance to the grains. The *faba*, the most useful kind of pulse, was evidently some variety of bean. It was often sown without any intermediate ploughing on land from which grain had been harvested, the seed being dropped apparently into the furrow between the ridges of stubble, which were then turned over upon it by the plough. When the beans were three inches high, they were banked up with the hoe, or else the board plough already described was run through between the rows, and afterwards they were two or three times cleared of weeds by the hoe — and this was the general manner of cultivating the other varieties of pulse.

The value of turnips (*rāpa*) as food for cattle and sheep was perfectly understood, and they were extensively raised.

**A few words may here be given to the subject of rotation of crops** as it was practised by the Roman farmer. Some of the richer parts of Campania bore a crop of grain every year. The elder Pliny mentions one field in the fork between the roads which diverged from Capua to Cumæ and Puteoli, which regularly bore spelt (*fār*) for two years, then panic [1] (*pānicum*) for one, and so on in perpetual rotation; but this was a prodigy even in fertile Campania. A recurrent succession of barley (*hordeum*), millet (*milium*), and turnips was more common, though this demanded a rich soil, and it was customary to manure for the millet when its turn came round. Another expedient was alternating spelt and spring beans, manuring the latter. Less fertile land lay fallow every

[1] Panic, though exhausting, was a summer grain

third year, common soil on alternate years, this being
the method recommended by Virgil; and certain crops,
such as lupine (*lupīnus*), were sown merely to be ploughed
in as a fertilizer.

There was always a vegetable garden (*hortus olitōrius*)
on the Roman farm, where were to be found a great
variety of pot-herbs (*herbae pulmentāriae*), lettuce (*lac
tūca*), and other salads, cabbages (*brassicae*) of many
kinds, leeks (*porrum*) and onions (*caepa*), carrots
(*pastināca*) and turnips (*rāpa*), asparagus and artichokes
(*cardus*), beans (*faba*) and peas (*pīsum*), cucumbers
(*cucumis*) and melons (*mēlo*).

**Market-gardening** was a flourishing industry, and the
raising of flowers, notably violets and roses, provided a
town were within easy reach, was strongly recommended.
But the olive and the grape were, after all, the two most
characteristic Roman crops.

If ten per cent was a fair interest on money invested
in a vineyard, as Columella asserts, it is curious that
viticulture should have gone even temporarily out of
fashion, as it seems to have done at one period in the
early days of the Empire. Then, as now, the soil preferred for a vineyard was gravelly, and, in starting a
fresh one, new ground was broken if possible, or, at all
events, that which had never borne vines before. That
the young plants should be of good stock, was, of course,
the first necessity; then a thorough and repeated working of the soil was required, and a careful cutting back
of the shoots and roots of the vines.

**Practically, there were but two ways of training vines,** —
on trellises and on trees. In the former case, the main
stock of the vine was trained up a pole to the height of

five or six feet, where it was allowed to branch, and here
a cross-bar (*iŭgum*) was fastened to the pole. Over this
the branches were thrown, and carried back to the ground,
where they rooted, and formed new stock to replenish
the vineyard. Among trees to which the vine might be
trained, the elm was preferred, and Virgil announces in
the very opening of the Georgics, that an important part
of his pleasing task will be to describe the art of "marry-
ing the vine to the elm."

Its leaves, which had to be plucked in order to give
sunshine to the grapes, were an excellent food for cattle;
it grew easily in most soils, and could be severely
trimmed without diminishing its vitality. When a tree
was intended as the support of a vine, its trunk was
kept smooth for eight feet above the ground. Three
equidistant branches were then left, and the same number was allowed to grow, at intervals of three feet, to
the top of the tree, care being always taken that the
members of the successive layers should not come
directly above one another.

The vines were set at varying distances apart, according to the quality of the soil, the nature of the climate,
and the mode in which they were to be trained. Columella says [1] that nobody can help getting a *culleus* [2] of
wine from a *iŭgerum;* but in all cases the soil is required
to be incessantly worked. From spring to winter the
ground was spaded over at least once a month. One man
was supposed equal to the care of seven *iŭgera*, and the
fettered slaves appear to have been often appointed to
this task. At the vintage, of course, extra labor was
called in. On the nineteenth of August, the *Vīnālia*

[1] De Re Rus. iii. 3.          [2] See Table.

*Rūstica*, sacrifices were offered to Jupiter, and the *flāmen diālis*, with much solemnity, broke a bunch of grapes from a vine-branch, and declared the vintage begun. Practically, however, grapes appear to have been gathered as they ripened, without much regard to this festival; only no new wine might be taken into the city until after it had occurred.

**Long before the grapes were gathered,** the vintner must see that all the utensils were ready for the wine-making, cleanly washed and rinsed in salted, or, better still, in sea-water, while vessels of clay were, if necessary, daubed inside with pitch to render them impervious.

The grapes were first trodden by the feet, then twice pressed, and the final refuse, mixed with water, formed the beverage called *lora*, which was the winter drink of the slaves. If the must were to be kept sweet, jars were filled with it, tightly covered, then sunk in sand or water for a month or six weeks, after which it was warranted to remain unaltered in taste for a year at least. Much of the must was boiled down into a jelly used for flavoring and preserving poor wines. This boiling down was a most delicate operation. It was done by night in a great leaden vessel (brass and copper were thought to impart an unpleasant flavor), over a fire, slow at first, and then brisker, the liquid being constantly stirred to prevent burning, and carefully skimmed of all impurities. The resultant jelly received different names, *dēfrutum*, *sapa*,[1] etc., according to the proportion of the original must which had been boiled away.

The rest of the must was taken to the wine-cellar (*cella vīnāria*) and put into the *dōlia*, huge earthen jars

[1] Whence the Italian *sapa* and French *sabe*.

holding rather more than a hundred gallons. Here the must was allowed to ferment, and here it was doctored with the various ingredients used to flavor and preserve it. The chief of these were boiled-down must (*dēfrutum*, etc.), sea-water which had been bottled, and kept a number of years, lime, turpentine, and pitch. Aromatic herbs and spices were also sometimes employed.

Dolium (Rich).

The *cella vīnāria* was constructed with a dry earthen bed, and if the wine were weak, the *dōlia* were sunk deeply in the earth. Fermentation required about nine days, after which the *dōlia* were tightly covered and only looked at from time to time.

The common wines were drunk directly from the *dōlia*, and from these were also filled the ox- and goat-skins in which wine was transported to a distance. Finer wines were always bottled off in *amphorae*, with all sorts of superstitious precautions, and stored away, not as with us in the cellar, but in a dry room at the top of the house (*apothēca*).

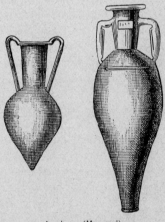

Amphorae (Marquard).

Thus Horace in his gay ode to the Amphora,[1] calls upon

[1] Hor. Od. iii. 21.

the jar of choice Massic wine to *come down* from its place of rest and help him celebrate the festival of his friend Messala Corvinus. Sweet wines were also made from sun-dried grapes, and innumerable liqueurs of which wine formed the basis.

**Although the season of olive-gathering** came earlier in Roman days than now in Italy, oil was not made till the vintage was well over. The best way of all was to pick the olive by hand, but where this was impracticable they were gently beaten from the tree with osier-rods.

From the pulp of the olive were and are expressed two liquids, — oil proper, and that thin, watery fluid, dark and bitter, which was called *amurca* by the Romans, and used by them as manure. This came away from the olive with much less pressure than the oil, or else it oozed from the berry after it was gathered; and many farmers left the olives spread out upon a dry, sloping floor, for two or three days before they were pressed, on purpose to allow the *amurca* to run away and a slight fermentation to take place. Others considered this practice most injurious to the fruit. In any case the berries were carefully picked over, and each day's harvest not only cleaned by itself, but kept distinct during all the processes of oil-making. In general, the gentler the pressure to which the olive-pulp was subjected, the better the resultant oil, which was roughly divided into three grades. It was cleared of *amurca* by being poured from one pan to another, often to the number of thirty, after having been allowed to stand for a while and settle in each. In very cold weather, when the oil and *amurca* could not be separated in this way, a little salt or nitre was mixed with the liquid. When thoroughly clarified, the oil was put into *dōlia* and tightly corked. Throughout its making the oil must have been carefully protected from the touch of smoke, which was thought as deleterious in this case as desirable for new-made wine.

Olives were also pickled and preserved in a variety of ways; and since the olive-tree commonly bore only every other year, it was customary to have two orchards furnishing alternate harvests. Once fairly started, an olive orchard demanded comparatively little labor; the ground about the trees was annually dug or ploughed, the suckers trimmed, and the roots cut back; but the trees were manured only every third year, and their branches trimmed once in eight or even more; on the year they did not bear, some other crop was raised between the trees.

Grafting was a common practice with all fruit-trees, the Roman method being substantially the same as our own.

In considering the Roman farmer's year as a whole, we find that he computed rainy days and festivals at forty-five, and reckoned on thirty days after the sowing when there was no field labor to be done. But on these thirty days, and on the stormy ones, there were ropes to make, baskets to weave, and other home-made utensils to prepare; while all the other implements of the husbandman — his "mute servants," as Varro[1] calls them — had to be repaired and thoroughly cleaned. Even on feast-days certain kinds of work were allowed, such as the clearing of drains and the mending of highways, so that only the December Saturnalia seem to have afforded a complete holiday to the slaves.

[1] Varr. Re Rus. i. 17.

On New Year's day, a little work of every kind was done for good luck; but then followed a time of comparative relaxation. In the latter half of January, the ground was cleared of brambles, and the trimming of the vineyards completed; while the autumn-sown grain and the beans, if they were sufficiently grown, were hoed for the first time. Early trees were now grafted, and the stock was planted. Vineyards were also cultivated, and young orchards set out, grass sown and ground broken, fields manured and osier-beds renewed. Vine-sets were also transplanted, if needful, and the late fruit-trees grafted.

In March, the vegetable garden was prepared, the autumn grains received their second hoeing, and the spring grains were sown. In April, came weeding, sheep-washing, the setting out of new vineyards, the trimming of old vines, and the olive-grafting.

May brought the earliest mowing, and in this month the earth was first spaded up about the olive-trees, and the vineyards dug over, this latter process being repeated each month until cold weather. The olives were also trimmed, the vine-shoots nipped; in warmer latitudes the sheep were shorn, and the lupins, which had been sown as fertilizer, were ploughed in. In June the first ploughing was finished and the second done, the threshing-floor was made ready, vetches mown, beans picked, and honey taken from the hives.

Grain-harvest took place in July, and the cutting of the straw and gathering of leaves for the winter fodder of cattle. In August, figs and grapes were dried for winter use, and brakes cut for litter.

September was, *par excellence*, the month of the vintage, and then, too, turnips were planted, and the later grains harvested. In October, winter grains were sown and harrowed in, trees trimmed, and the olive-picking begun.

November was devoted to a general cleaning-up of autumn work. The making of oil was finished in December, and the vines trained, and we may close the brief *résumé* of the work of the Roman agricultural year by a few general precepts from the Natural History of the elder Pliny [1]: " He is no farmer who buys what his estate can supply. He is a bad head of a household who does by day what can be done by night, — except in case of foul weather; he is a worse who does on working-days what is permitted on holidays; the worst of all is he who on a pleasant day chooses to work within doors rather than in the field."

[1] Plin. Nat. Hist. xviii. 6.

# CHAPTER VI.

## TRAVEL, TRANSPORTATION, AMUSEMENTS.

WHEN Rome was at the summit of her power, the entire extent of the Empire was provided with a system of public highways which rendered communication between the different parts of Europe easy and comparatively rapid. Three principal post-roads diverged from Rome, starting from three separate gates. From the Porta Capena,[1] at the southeastern angle of the city wall, the Via Appia ran over the Alban hills, and across the Pontine Marshes to Capua, where it divided. The right-hand branch led to Rhegium (Reggio), and thence by ferry to Messina and the principal cities of Sicily, one of which, Lilybæum (Capo di Boco), was the regular port of winter departure for Carthage and Africa. In summer the direct sea-passage from Ostia was usually preferred. From Carthage, roads of Roman construction led westward and communicated with Spain, and eastward to Asia, and also penetrated for some distance into the interior.

The left-hand road from Capua went to Brundusium (Brindisi). From this point, a twenty-four hours' voyage brought the traveller to Dyrrachium (Durazzo in European

---

[1] After the building of the Aurelian wall, from the Porta Appia, fifteen hundred yards further out.

Turkey), whence he might follow the Egnatian Way through Illyria, Macedonia, and Thrace to Constantinople; while branch roads led to other important points, and especially to Athens, and to Antioch, which was the centre of Eastern trade. Brundusium was also connected by a coast road with Ariminum (Rimini), the terminus of the Flaminian Way.

This very important road left Rome by the Porta Flaminia, on or near the site of the present Porta del Popolo, crossed the Tiber at the Mulvian bridge, where is now the Ponte Molle, and ran northward through mid-Italy, by way of Narnia and Spoletum (Narni and Spoleto) to Rimini, as aforesaid. From this point another coast road ran northward to Aquileia, — the starting-point for the Danubian provinces; while the Via Æmilia turned westerly and led by way of Bologna and Modena (Bononia and Mutina) to Milan (Mediolanum). From Modena, another great road led northward to Verona and the Brenner Pass.

The main highway to Western Europe was unquestionably the Aurelian, which struck the Mediterranean at Centum Cellæ (Civita Vecchia), and followed the coast from there as far as Arelas (Arles), in the Provincia, which was a seaport in Roman times, and from which point, Spain, France, and Britain were all easily reached. There was also certainly a way from Milan into Gaul by the passes of the Alps, though its exact course can no longer be determined. Traces of Roman work have, in fact, been found on nearly every Alpine pass now in use, and the "Itineraries" plainly mention those of Mont Genèvre, the Great and the Little St. Bernard, and the Splügen. There was another great system of highways which connected Germany, Northern France, and England.

**The model for all these mighty roads was the oldest and most frequented of them all, the Via Appia.** Originally built by Appius Claudius in 312 B.C., it was restored and virtually reconstructed by the emperors Nerva and Trajan; and it was their road which, in the sixth century A.D., excited the wonder and admiration of Procopius, who found it broad enough for two teams to pass abreast, and paved with large blocks of foreign stone, so accurately fitted that no joining was visible. It is hardly probable that all the highroads we have enumerated were as magnificently constructed as the Appian Way, yet the time made by the regular post does not seem greatly to have varied on the different routes, and was everywhere much the same as that of the modern *diligence*.

**The speed of government couriers** was reckoned, for long distances, at something over one hundred English miles a day.[1] Private travelling, by hired conveyance, was necessarily slower. Cæsar, indeed, Plutarch tells us, accomplished the journey from Rome to the Rhone (796 Roman miles) within eight days, but then Cæsar's journeys were considered miracles of celerity. The private travellers of later times could sometimes make use of the government post, but only by special imperial permission.

Private letters were usually conveyed by foot-runners, or *tabellāriī*, who made about twenty-five Roman miles a day, covering, for example, the 124 miles from Rome to Capua in about five days.

[1] The journey from Antioch to Constantinople, for example, 747 Roman miles, occupied not quite six days.

**Mānsiōnēs, or night quarters,** for the bearers of dispatches, were to be found at similar intervals, that is, about twenty-five Roman miles apart, and they must, in most instances, have been quite regularly distributed, since we find their number used as a measure of distance. Halting-places of a more sumptuous nature were provided for the Emperor and his especial deputies.

The support of the roads, as well as of the post-system of earlier times, fell entirely upon the districts through which the roads passed; and though some portion of this expense was later transferred to the imperial treasury, it always remained a heavy charge upon the provinces.

No public provision was made for private travellers, their needs being met by individual enterprise. There were men in most Italian cities who let out *raedae*, which were rather roomy four-wheeled carriages, and *cisia*, a species of light two-wheeled gig, as well as the horses

Cisium (Rich).

or mules to draw them. The offices of these *cisiāriī* or *iūmentāriī*, were at the city-gates, — for driving within the walls was almost unknown, — and here the bargain was made either for changing carriage and horses from stage to stage, or for making the whole journey with the same team. Doubtless a man might also use his own conveyance, if he had one, with the horses or mules to be hired along the road.

In the latter days of the Republic, great pomp began

to be affected by wealthy travellers, and this increased to such a pitch that Nero's regular train consisted of a thousand wagons, while Poppæa took along with her five hundred she-asses for convenience of bathing in their milk, and tipped her horses' shoes with gold.

Seneca[1] observes satirically that "everybody travels nowadays with a troop of Numidian cavalry in front, and a band of scouts sent on ahead. . . . They all have mules, loaded with vessels of glass and murrha, and sculptured by the hand of famous craftsmen, for it would be beneath a man's dignity to load his packs with articles which would bear knocking about." And he also tells us, with true Stoic vanity, that he once made a two days' journey with a friend, attended by so few servants that a single vehicle sufficed for them all.

**The traveller of consequence avoided, if possible, passing a single night in any inn.** On the incessantly frequented route from Rome to Naples, he was almost sure either to have a villa of his own, or a friend whose hospitality he might demand. Failing these, he would take tents along and camp out, if the season were sufficiently mild, and doubtless it was the absence of distinguished patronage which made the inn of those days both so comfortless and so cheap. It is certain, however, that places of public entertainment, such as they were (*dēversōria, tabernae, meritōria*), existed all along the most frequented roads of the Empire, and that they were, in some cases, aided from the treasury. Neighboring proprietors often built them on speculation, letting them to a landlord, or managing them through their own slaves. At certain

[1] See Ep. cxxiii. 6.

places there would be a choice of inns, and Horace remarks [1] on the rival establishments of Forum Appii.
*Popīnae,* or restaurants, both *popīnae sellāriolae* where a
regular table was laid, and the humbler kind where a
lunch was taken standing, are mentioned so often as
to lead us to infer, that the fashion of renting furnished
rooms (*meritōriae*) and going out for one's meals was
as common in ancient Rome as in Latin countries now.

In the rural inns it was always customary to pay a
lump sum for board and lodging, and, indeed, one hardly
sees how items could have been specified, when the total
bill amounted to a half as, which Polybius says [2] was the
regular charge in his days for one night's entertainment
in the inns of Cisalpine Gaul.   Among the discoveries
at Pompeii is that of a tavern-sign on which is depicted
the hostess reckoning the dues of a departing guest, of
whom she demands for bread and wine one as, for other
food, two asses, and for mule's provender the same.

**Tavern-signs** appear to have been regularly used,
and birds and animals were favorite devices, from which,
as now, the tavern took its name, — at the sign of the
Stork, the Elephant, the great Eagle, the Camel, the
Raven.   Inscriptions were often painted on these signs,
urging the claims of the house upon the traveller, and
host or hostess would stand upon the threshold to solicit
the patronage of the passer-by.   The proverbial reputation of inn-keepers was very bad.   They were supposed,
as a matter of course, to water their wine, and steal the
fodder of the animals they stabled; and an impression
prevailed, exaggerated, one may hope, that they were
ready, not merely to murder such guests as were sup-

[1] Hor. Sat. i, 5, 4.          [2] Polyb. ii, 157.

posed to have valuables about them, but to eat them as
well. Galen, who repeats the charge, appends by way
of ghastly commentary, and, as it would seem, from
experience, that human flesh tastes much like that of
swine. Even St. Augustine [1] confesses to having heard
tales, which, however, he declines implicitly to believe,
of Italian hostesses who put something into their cheeses,
which turned those who partook of these dainties into
beasts of burden, whom they then compelled to perform
certain tasks, restoring them to their human semblance
after these were completed.

**The customs-dues** appear to have been as much dreaded
as they are by the returning European traveller of our
own day, and there was a good deal of evasion on the one
side, and of rudeness on the other. Soldiers' luggage
was, however, free of duty, and a man's effects might be
exempted by especial favor of the Emperor, as were those
of the sophist Polemo of Smyrna, by Trajan.

**Highway robbers** abounded in the outlying provinces
of the Empire, in all mountainous districts, and especially
in the tract of forest which divided the Pontine marshes
from the sea. Military expeditions were frequently sent
against them, but without much permanent effect. When
Septimius Severus disbanded the Prætorian guard, a
good many of its members, and of the class from which
it had been recruited, "took to the road," as the English
phrase used to be; and toward the close of that Emperor's reign (that is to say, in the middle years of the
third century A.D.), there was a famous bandit, bearing
the obviously fictitious name of Felix Bulla, and com-
manding a band of six hundred men, whose history is an

[1] Aug. Civ. Dei xviii. 18.

opera ready made.  His principal headquarters were
in the neighborhood of Brindisi, where all tourists of
apparent affluence, arriving either from the West or the
East, were ordered to stand and deliver.  His force was
admirably organized, he was both bold and wary, and
long avoided capture, but was at length betrayed into
the hands of the Prefect Papinianus.  "How came you
to be a robber?" was the rather futile preliminary
inquiry of his judge, to which the captive replied, "How
came you to be a prefect?"[1]  Felix Bulla was thrown
to the beasts in the amphitheatre, but his race survived.
Those who went southward from Rome by day, during
the first century of our era, were, in general, safe enough,
owing to the very press of travel upon the road.  There
was a constant succession of those pompous caravans
described by Seneca, whose owners aped imperial luxury.
The expense thus incurred was often literally ruinous,
and some of those, who had thus flaunted upon the road,
ended their days as gladiators, a profession which Nero
had made rather fashionable.  For the time being,
however, the carriage horses of the ambitious tourist
were well matched and well bred, and their leathern
shoes were furnished with silver tips.  Otherwise, the
traveller made use of fast mules, which were no less
costly.  These animals had often rich purple housings,
heavily embroidered, while their harnesses were studded
with gold.  The wagons were sumptuously decorated
with gold and silver plates, on which the value of an
entire estate might easily be spent, while their cushions
and curtains were of silk or some equally expensive
stuff.

[1] Dio Cass. lxxvi.

**One of the vehicles most commonly used** was the *carpentum*. It had two wheels and an arched awning, and was, in fact, only a luxurious development of the common farm-cart, which bore the same name, — the cover having been added for protection against rain and sun. This was the kind of carriage affected by those great ladies in

Carpentum (Rich).

whose favor was first relaxed that prohibition of the use of wheeled vehicles inside the walls of Rome, which had remained in force throughout the republican period. When so occupied, the *carpentum*, and a variety of the same called a *pīlentum*, were always drawn by mules. They were so constructed as to hold two persons beside the driver. In the four-wheeled *raeda*, or *cārrūca*, the traveller had appliances for making himself most comfortable. Propped upon soft cushions, he whiled away the time with reading, writing, dice-throwing and other amusements. Martial advises the man who sets out on a long journey, to make Cicero his travelling companion, and the elder Pliny used to have both an amanuensis and a writing-table in his coach.

Smaller than the *carpentum*, but covered like it, and driven by the traveller himself, was the *covīnus*. There were also the open two-wheeled *essedum* and *cisium*, each of which had a single seat, accommodating the driver and one other person. The *cisium* seems, however, to have been lighter built, for the *essedum* was always drawn by a pair of animals, while the *cisium* had shafts, to one of which an extra horse was often attached, or, if great speed were desired, three animals would be harnessed abreast, as in the Russian *troïka*. The outside horses were called *fūnālēs*, or *fūnāriī*, from the rope with which they were attached to the *cisium*, much in the same manner as a third horse is attached to a street-car among ourselves. Five miles an hour was considered greet speed even for a *cisium*.

**Government couriers** usually rode one horse and led another. The Romans, until the fourth century, seem never to have used a saddle (*sella equestris*[1]); they rode either barebacked, or with a pad or cushion called the *ephippium*, similar to that always used by women, in which case, too, they seem to have ridden sidewise in feminine fashion. With or without the *ephippium*, the *strāgulum* (housing or caparison) was always used. It was often made of the skin of a beast with the

---

[1] Several kinds of pack-saddles, however, existed long before this date.

fur on, and sometimes of leather, which, for use in the army was covered with plates of metal, and served as a protection for the horse — Virgil[1] gives such a caparison, "covered with brazen scales like feathers," to the horse of Chlorus, the priest of Cybele, in the last battle for Latium. Housings of brightly colored woollen cloth were used for mere ornament, and a leathern band, adorned with plates of metal, often hung down over the breast. The general plan of the head-stall (*capistrum*) was very like ours; but whether for riding or driving, blinders and curb-bits were unknown. There was a special sort of invalid carriage in use at Rome from very early times, called *arcera*, from its resemblance to a large chest. The occupant lay within, upon cushions, while the driver was perched upon a little seat outside; but after the introduction of litters, the *arcera* was almost entirely superseded.

**The lectīca, or litter,** used at first merely for the transport of the sick or dead, became later the favorite travelling carriage for women. Its use by a man was long considered a mark of effeminacy, but in imperial times they became general. The wealth of the possessor of a *lectīca* was evinced, not only by the richness of its ornamentation, but by the number of bearers, two,

Lectica (Rich).

four, six, or eight. We do not know just how they carried their burden, only that, when set down, it rested

[1] Virg. Æn. xi. 770–771.

on four wooden legs. It also had a roof, supported at
the four corners, and there were curtains around the
sides, which could be drawn at pleasure; or else the
sides were shut in with windows made from plates of
alabaster, or other translucent stone, such as may still
be seen in some old Italian churches. The occupant
either reclined upon a heap of cushions, or the *lectīca*
was fitted with a feather bed. The *basterna* was a litter,
borne by two mules, one before and one behind. All
these conveyances were doubtless to be seen any fine
day on the Via Appia, as well as trains of sumpter-
mules (*dossuāriī, clītellāriī, sarcinālēs,* etc.), and heavy
carts bringing merchandise to the markets of Rome.

Except during the winter months, when the great
majority of vessels was laid up in harbor, the Roman
market was largely supplied by means of **the boat-service
on the Tiber,** from the harbors of Ostia and Portus
Trajani. A winter voyage is usually mentioned as a
thing of horror, but in the pleasant months of the year
it seems to have been a mode of travelling much favored
by the ancients, and more expeditious than journeying
by land. Although merchant vessels proper (*nāvēs
onerāriī*), such as those which brought the grain supply
from Egypt and Sicily, were propelled by sails alone, it
was in rowing that the Romans, like the Greeks, chiefly
excelled. How they managed their many banks of oars,
no modern is able perfectly to understand, and ships
with ten banks or more, must certainly have been mere
curiosities. There is even mention of one vessel with
forty banks, but three to five were the usual number, and
the Greek trireme could be depended upon to make eight
miles an hour. The voyage from Brundusium to Dyrra-

chium (Brindisi to Durazzo), with good wind and weather, might be accomplished in twenty-four hours, but what appliances the luxurious Roman had for making himself comfortable on shipboard, even during this brief transit, we do not know. Cabins there were, in the hold of the vessel, and a tent-like contrivance was sometimes erected on deck, which would, doubtless, afford a pleasant and sufficient shelter on those starlit summer nights which were chosen by preference for the crossing to Illyria and other short trips. On the coasting vessels, both sails and oars were used, and they could make a speed of six to eight nautical miles an hour.

The Romans were, upon the whole, great travellers, and their customary journeys may be classed under the three heads of business, instruction, and pleasure. Seldom, if ever, has the world seen a more thoroughly organized and extensive commercial system, than that which had its focus in Rome, in the first centuries of our era. Never, of a certainty, since that time, has the same current coin been used over so vast a stretch of territory. Local coinage of silver and copper, for local purposes, there doubtless was, in many of the provinces; but, except in Egypt, where the Greek *drachma* always held its own, the Roman *dēnārius* became the monetary unit throughout the Empire. It seems, also, to have passed current among the neighboring independent nations, as a Bank of England note will do to-day upon the Continent of Europe. Tacitus [1] remarks, however, that the Germans always gave the preference to those silver coins with the stamp of the *bīga*, which had prevailed before Nero's day, and to which they were accustomed, while

[1] Tac. Ger. 5.

they looked with suspicion on later coinages. As for gold, all articles of merchandise were so cheap in Germany, that that metal was seldom required.

Like the merchant of the Middle Ages, his Roman predecessor seems to have travelled in person to the markets where he desired to buy or sell. Horace makes many allusions to the trader who "tempts the wintry sea, moving continually to and fro between the equator and the pole"; and Manilius describes the same adventurer as buying up the produce of the world, carrying his own wares into unknown lands, and ever acquiring fresh treasures under novel suns. These apparently poetic statements are corroborated by the monumental inscription of a merchant found at Hierapolis, which sets forth that he made seventy-two crossings between Malea on the Peloponnesos and Italy, while one C. Oc. Agathopus, declares upon his own gravestone at Pozzuoli, that, wearied out with travelling from East to West, he has here found repose at last. These merchant-voyages were not confined to the Mediterranean and Black Sea, but extended to the Atlantic, to the ports of Spain, France, England, and, very possibly, Ireland. The conquest of Egypt also opened the way to the East Indies. The regular route of the merchant led him first to Alexandria, starting whence in summer, he struck the mouth of the Nile, and sailed up that stream to Coptos, — a twelve days' voyage with favorable winds. At Coptos, his wares were transferred to the backs of camels, and the caravan set out for the shores of the Red Sea. Moving only by night, on account of the intense heat, and resting all day, it took nearly a fortnight to reach the coast, with which the Ptolomean canal formed another means of communication. In Strabo's time, a fleet of a hundred and twenty vessels plied constantly between Myoshormos, a Red Sea port, lying nearly opposite Mt. Sinai and the extremity of Arabia Petræa, and India; and each of these vessels, Pliny further informs us, had a company of archers on board, to protect the cargo against pirates. A voyage of thirty days brought the vessels either to Ocelis (Acila), in Arabia, at the lower extremity of the Red Sea, or to Cane, on the south coast of Arabia. It was forty days' journey hence, to the coast of Malabar, which, however, was in such bad repute for safety, that it was customary to prolong the voyage to a more southerly point. The whole expedition, from Alexandria to India and back, occupied from six to seven months, that is to say, from midsummer to some time in the following February. The incredible number of Roman coins found in India, testifies clearly enough to the extent of the Indo-Roman commerce. There is, indeed, some reason to suppose that a certain *dēnārius*, bearing the image of Augustus, with his adopted sons, Lucius and Gaius, was struck off for this trade only.

**The importations** from the East were much the same in Roman times as now, — silk, spices, pearls, ivory, and gold. The article of commerce most sought in the markets of Northern Europe was amber (*ēlectrum* or *sūcinum*), for which there was a great demand among the Romans, and, in quest of which the merchants often went far beyond the boundary of the Roman Empire. Tacitus tells [1] of a colony of Roman merchants, which the army ran across in Bohemia, who confessed that they had come there first in hopes of gain, and then

[1] Tac. Ann. ii. 62.

stayed on, till the new ties formed in this barbarous land had grown stronger than the old. There was also an excellent opening for trade in Gaul, whose inhabitants were always ready to give a slave for a cask of wine.

Wherever a permanent camp of Roman soldiers was established, the Roman merchant speedily found his way, and it would be hard to say which formed the more effective missionary of Roman civilization. Foreign merchants also visited Italy in large numbers, especially those of the Orient, which last came, in the process of time, so to throng all ports of the Empire, that in the fifth century Syrian and merchant appear to have become synonymous terms. "Here," writes[1] the Bishop Sidonius Apollinaris from Ravenna, in his whimsical description of that venerable city as a place where everything is topsy-turvy, "here priests let out money at usury, and Syrians sing psalms."

After Rome, the most important commercial centres were Corinth, Alexandria, and Arles, and certain places appear also then, as now, to have had a monopoly of the trade in certain articles. Thus Alexandria was said to supply the whole world with glass and paper, and Spain sent shiploads of quince marmalade in all directions. The Romans imported their beloved fish sauces largely from Antibes, and preferred the fine linen of Berytus (Beyrout) to that of any other make.

**Great stress was laid upon travel** as putting a finishing touch to the education of a distinguished youth, whose mind was supposed to be expanded by the mere sight of novel scenes. Rich young Romans were sent to study (theoretically) for a year or more away from home,

[1] Sid. Ap. Ep. i. 1.

either in some Italian city or preferably in Greece. Often they followed from place to place some philosopher whose tenets they had embraced; for the rhetoricians and sophists were perpetually on the move, and their nomad life was adopted by other classes of people. Not only quack-doctors, but physicians in good and regular standing, travelled about the world, and took pride in the breadth of their experience. So also did portrait-painters and skilled artisans of all kinds, and unquestionably there were numbers of strolling troupes of actors, musicians, and athletes.

A sea-voyage and change of air were favorite prescriptions with the physicians of those days, and recommended for almost all ailments, — pulmonary weakness, habitual pain in the head, low spirits, and paralysis. Egypt was one of the favorite health resorts; a residence among pine-woods was often recommended; milk cures were to be found at many seaside resorts, such as Stabiæ (Castellamare), whilst almost all the medicated springs we know were frequented in Roman times.

There were also many religious pilgrimages to the temples of distinguished divinities, or to oracles of old and high repute; while on occasions like that of the Olympic games in Greece, or any particularly gorgeous gladiatorial show at Rome, the influx of pilgrims from abroad was often tremendous.

**The Roman also travelled as a mere tourist,** most of all to Greece, whose beautiful monuments every self-respecting citizen of the later Republic felt that he ought once, at least, to have seen. There could hardly be a Grecian town so insignificant as not to boast some temple which, over and above its religious character, partook of

that of a museum, with glorious works of art dating
from the greatest period, and relics of demi-gods and
heroes. Though somewhat shamefaced about accepting
them implicitly, the Roman traveller was always deeply
interested in objects which claimed connection with that
great epic war under the walls of Troy, which had led to
the building of Rome. Enthusiasts in this line even
went to Asia Minor on an express hunt for Trojan relics,
while Egypt, after its conquest, attracted larger and
larger numbers of the curious year by year. The traveller of classic times had few guide-books, but he could
hardly reach a city where he would not find a living
guide prepared to take him about, and show him all that
was worth seeing. These *valets-de-place*, though not yet
called by the name of the most versatile of Romans, were
often antiquarians of education and position.

But while the Roman of the Augustan Age had often
a highly cultivated taste in the matter of art, his enjoy-
ment of the beauties of nature was much more limited.
Those grander aspects and phenomena of the outer world,
which are so thrilling to the modern mind, were simply
uncomfortable and repugnant to him; and this is probably why, despite his love of change and restless desire
to enlarge his borders, the Roman was never a very
ardent explorer. Certain of the gentler aspects and
humbler charms of nature — cool springs with mossy
banks, broad, green meadows and quiet sheets of water,
shady groves and fair garden-beds — he did love intensely,
as countless passages in the Latin poets show; and such
he would have about his country-house, or if, like
Atticus, he were rich enough, even in the city. But his
villa was his first extravagance, and always his peculiar

pet and pride. "In all the length and breadth of this
Empire," says Seneca,[1] "there is no lake whose borders
are not studded with the roofs of Roman nobles, no river-
bank where they have not built." All along the Mediterranean, far south from Ostia, these villas lined the
coast, crowding close upon one another at favorite sites,
like Baiæ. The inland estates, like those of the younger
Pliny, near the sources of the Tiber in Umbria (the
modern Città di Castello), were of much greater extent;
but even so, they were almost continuous.

It is difficult to say how many distinct properties a
Roman of rank might not possess in late republican or
early imperial times. If Cicero and Pliny, who have told
as so much about their various installations, are to be
taken as representative cases, one would say that four or
five huge country-seats, and as many lesser villas, would
be a moderate allowance, while the dates of the letters of
these two show how incessantly they moved from one
place to another. Sometimes, no doubt, they did so at
the bidding of their affairs. Often they were impelled
by mere restlessness and love of change.

"Hence are vague journeyings undertaken," says
Seneca[2] in his discourse on Tranquillity of Spirit, "and
divers coasts are visited, but everywhere, whether on
land or on sea, we discover that levity of mind which is
always disgusted with the present. Now we seek Campania, and anon, growing disgusted with its delicacies,
we make for the wilderness and explore the forests of
Bruttium and Lucania. But the craving for something
pleasant revives in the desert, and our dainty eyes must
needs have some relief from the tedious squalor of those

[1] Sen. Ep. lxxxix. 21.      [2] Sen. De Tran. An. ii.

rude spots. Tarentum is the place ! — we praise its harbor, its exquisite winter climate, and its fine old mansions. Finally we bend our steps toward the city of cities. Too long have our ears missed the din of the streets, the plaudits of the theatre. We are ready even for a taste of human blood. Thus journey follows journey, and scene succeeds to scene, and so it is, as the poet Lucretius says, that 'every man would from himself escape.'"

The restless being described in this passage was, of course, a spoiled child of fortune, but never at any period of his history was the Roman very ingenious in devising for himself home amusements and simple recreations. It was not quite natural for him to play. The mimes and songs and dances of primitive times had almost all a religious significance. They appeal to the gods, and were laudatory or propitiatory in their character. There are, indeed, allusions in Virgil's roseate picture of the good old times to something like the rustic sports of "Merrie England," — "leaping upon greased and inflated hides, in the fair meadows," and the like ; [1] and Cicero and Suetonius both speak of casting lots by means of the game called "*micāre digitīs*," which consisted of throwing out under cover a certain number of fingers for your adversary to guess, and which was much the same as the *mora* of modern Italy. But even these elementary amusements, though ancient, were, perhaps, not indigenous, while the dramatic representations and games of the circus, which came to exercise so enthralling a fascination over the town-bred Roman of later times, were certainly an importation from Greece. These monster shows however, of which the great majority were organ-

[1] Virg. Geor. ii. 382.

ized and exhibited for political purposes, belong to the
public rather than the private life of the Roman.

**It remains to say a few words concerning the games of
children and youths.** The former, like the rising genera-
tion always and everywhere, had their dolls and their
hobby-horses, their toy houses and carts. They skipped
stones, they spun tops (*turbinēs*), they walked upon stilts
(*grāllae*). They had also active games of emulation or
skill, in which the best fellow won, and Horace quotes
in his first epistle, the boys who say, "If you beat, you
shall be king" (*rēx eris, sī rēctē faciēs*), while the rather
vulgar catchword of a boys' foot race, "*occupet extrēmum
scabiēs*" (a murrain seize the hindmost), is applied by
the same humorous author in his Ars Poetica to the
freaks of a too froward literary ambition.

Nuts were such very favorite playthings with a Roman
boy, that the expression *nucēs relinquere* came to be
synonymous with the putting away of childish things, as
we have already seen in the case of the young bridegroom, of whom largess of nuts was demanded by the
*gamins* who followed his bridal procession. Many different games were played with these cheap and convenient
counters, such as the *lūdus castellōrum*, which required
four nuts, of which three had to be so arranged that the
fourth could be balanced upon, without displacing them ;
which done, all the four accrued to the deft player; and
the game of *pār impār*, which explains itself, being precisely the universal "odd or even?"

The youth who had outgrown nuts or marbles played
ball, either by himself, with one, two, or three balls, or
with one or more associates, who had to play by turn
(*datātim lūdere*), and must be equally expert in throwing

(*dare* or *mittere*), catching (*excipere*), and returning (*re-mittere* or *repercutere*). The *trigōn* was a triangular game of ball sufficiently dignified to be played upon the Campus Martius by grown men, and difficult enough to require much practice. The chief peculiarity of the *trigōn* was that the balls were not delivered in regular order, but flung to any player at the caprice of the server, and each of the three players had to catch and throw simultaneously. The *sphaeromachia* was a still more elaborate game of ball, in which the players took sides, and their ground was marked out somewhat as for lawn-tennis.

Children of a yet larger growth amused themselves with the innumerable games of hazard which depend upon the throwing of dice (*tesserae* or *tālī*). *Tesserae* were cubical, and marked exactly like the dice of to-day. They were shaken upon a flat surface from a cup or dice-box, which went by many names, — *turricula*, *fritillus*, *ōrca*. Three dice were usually thrown, and the high-

est throw was, of course, triple sixes. *Tālī* were originally made from the ankle-bones of animals, whence their name. They were numbered upon four sides only, being rounded on the other two.

Fritillus (Rich).

Four was the number regularly thrown, and the highest cast, called *Venus*, was that in which the four different numbers, one, three, four, and six came uppermost (two and five were never marked upon *tālī*). There were also several games played with *calculī* (balls or pellets) upon a board (*tabula*), a favorite one being the so-called *lūdus latrun-*

*culārius,* which bore some faint resemblance to chess, and where victory seems to have consisted in capturing and disabling as many thieves (*latrōnēs*) as possible. But war was, after all, the Roman's favorite pastime, and no manner of contest upon a mimic field commanded his ardent interest.

# APPENDIX.

## I.

### A. Smaller Measures.

| | | |
|---|---|---|
| Digitus . . . . . . . . . | = | .7281 in. |
| 1⅓ Digiti = Uncia . . . . . . . . . . | = | .9708 in. |
| 4 Digiti or 3 Unciae = Palmus . . . . . | = | 2.9124 in. |
| 3 Palmi = Palmus Major (late) . . . . . | = | 8.7372 in. |
| 4 Palmi = Pes . . . . . . . . . . . | = | 11.6496 in. |
| 5 Palmi = Palmipes . . . . . . . . . | = | 1 ft. 2.562  in. |
| 6 Palmi = Cubitus . . . . . . . . . | = | 1 ft. 5.4744 in. |

### B. Larger Measures.

| | | |
|---|---|---|
| Pes . . . . . . . . . . | = | 11.6496 in. |
| 2½ Pedes = Gradus . . . . . . . | = | 2 ft. 5.124  in. |
| 2 Gradus = Passus . . . . . . . | = | 4 ft. 10.248  in. |
| 2 Passus = Decempeda or Pertica . . | = | 9 ft. 8.496  in. |
| 12 Perticae = Actus [1] . . . . . . . | = 116 ft. 5.952  in. |
| 1000 Passus = Mille Passuum . . . . | = 4854 ft. = .9193 mile. |

## II.

### ROMAN SQUARE MEASURE.

| | | |
|---|---|---|
| Pes Quadratus = | | .94245 sq. ft. |
| 480 Ped. Quad. = Actus Simplex = | | 1 sq. R. 180.127 sq. ft. |
| 5 Act. Simp. = Uncia [2] = | | 8 sq. R. 83.885 sq. ft. |
| 6 Unciae = Actus Quadratus = | 1 rood | 9 sq. R. 231.07 sq. ft. |
| 2 Act. Quad. = Iugerum [3] = | 2 roods | 19 sq. R. 189.89 sq. ft. |

[1] The *Actus* was the regulation length of furrow in ploughing with oxen, and was to be drawn without breathing space.

[2] That is twelfth part of Iugerum.

[3] Or very nearly five-eighths of our acre.

## III.

### ROMAN LIQUID MEASURE.

|  |  |  |  |  |  |
|---|---|---|---|---|---|
|  | Ligula . . . . . . . . = |  |  |  | .024 pts. |
| 4 Ligulae | = Cyathus (Uncia of Sextarius) = |  |  |  | .096 pts. |
| 3 Cyathi | = Quartarius ($\frac{3}{12}$ " " ) = |  |  |  | .289 pts. |
| 2 Quartarii | = Hemina ($\frac{6}{12}$ " " ) = |  |  |  | .578 pts. |
| 2 Heminae | = Sextarius . . . . . . = |  |  |  | 1.155 pts. |
| 6 Sextarii | = Congius . . . . . . . = | 3 qts. | .934 pts. |
| 4 Congii | = Urna . . . . . . . . = | 13 qts. | 1.735 pts. |
| 2 Urnae | = Amphora . . . . . . . = | 27 qts. | 1.471 pts. |
| 20 Amphorae | = Culeus . . . . . = | 138 gal. | 2 qts. | 1.53 pts. |

## IV.

### ROMAN DRY MEASURE.

|  |  |  |  |  |
|---|---|---|---|---|
|  | Sextarius [1] = . . . . . . |  |  | .993 pts. |
| 8 Sextarii | = Semimodius = . . . . . . | 3 qts. | 1.944 pts. |
| 2 Semimodii | = Modius [2] = . . . . . . | 7 qts. | 1.888 pts. |

## V.

### ROMAN WEIGHTS.

#### A.  Uncial Divisions of the As.

|  |  |  | Grammes. | Oz. | Grains (Avoir ). |
|---|---|---|---|---|---|
|  | Uncia [3] . . . . . = | | 27.288 = | | 421.108 |
| 1½ Unciae | = Sescuncia . . . . . = | | 40.932 = | 1 | 194.163 |
| 1⅓ Sescuncia | = Sextans = | 2 unciae = | 54.576 = | 1 | 404.716 |
| 1½ Sextantes | = Quadrans = | 3 unciae = | 81.864 = | 2 | 388.324 |
| 1⅓ Quadrantes | = Triens = | 4 unciae = | 109.152 = | 3 | 371.932 |
| 1¼ Trientes | = Quincunx = | 5 unciae = | 136.44 = | 4 | 355.54 |

[1] The Sextarius of dry and liquid measure was of the same capacity, and the same subdivisions were made use of.

[2] Or, for rough calculation, the Modius equals the peck, and the Sextarius the pint.

[3] The Uncia differs from the ounce avoirdupois (437.5 grains) by 16.392 grains.

| | | | | Grammes. | Oz. | Grains (Avoir.). |
|---|---|---|---|---|---|---|
| $1\frac{1}{5}$ Quincunces | = Semis | = | 6 unciae | = 163.728 | = 5 | 339.148 |
| $1\frac{1}{6}$ Semes | = Septunx | = | 7 unciae | = 191.016 | = 6 | 322.756 |
| $1\frac{1}{2}$ Septunces | = Bes | = | 8 unciae | = 218.304 | = 7 | 306.364 |
| $1\frac{1}{8}$ Besses | = Dodrans | = | 9 unciae | = 245.592 | = 8 | 289.972 |
| $1\frac{1}{9}$ Dodrantes | = Dextans | = | 10 unciae | = 272.88 | = 9 | 273.580 |
| $1\frac{1}{10}$ Dextantes | = Deunx | = | 11 unciae | = 300.16 | = 10 | 257.188 |
| $1\frac{1}{11}$ Deunces | = As (Libra) | = | 12 unciae | = 327.45 | = 11 | 240.796 |

## B. Divisions of the Uncia.

| | | | | Grammes. | | Grains. (Avoir.). |
|---|---|---|---|---|---|---|
| | | Siliqua | = | .189 | = | 2.924 |
| 3 Siliquae | = | Obolus | = | .568 | = | 8.773 |
| 2 Oboli | = | Scrupulum | = | 1.137 | = | 17.546 |
| 2 Scrupula | = | Semisextula | = | 2.274 | = | 35.092 |
| 3 Scrupula | = | Drachma | = | 3.411 | = | 52.638 |
| 4 Scrupula | = | Sextula | = | 4.548 | = | 70.185 |
| 6 Scrupula | = | Sicilicus | = | 6.822 | = | 105.277 |
| 8 Scrupula | = | Duella | = | 9.096 | = | 140.369 |
| 12 Scrupula | = | Semuncia | = | 13.644 | = | 210.554 |
| 2 Semunciae | = | Uncia | = | 27.288 | = | 421.108 |
| 12 Unciae | = | As (Libra) | = | 327.45 | = | 5053.296 |

## VI.

### ROMAN MONEY.

#### A. B.C. 268–217.

| | | | | Weight in Grains (Avoir.). | | Value in Money. |
|---|---|---|---|---|---|---|
| | | As (copper) [1] | = | 1754.613 | = | \$.01968 |
| $2\frac{1}{2}$ Asses | = | Sestertius (silver) | = | 17.546 | = | \$.0492 |
| 2 Sestertii | = | Quinarius (silver) | = | 35.092 | = | \$.0984 |
| 2 Quinarii | = | Denarius (silver) [2] | = | 70.184 | = | \$.1968 |

[1] In still earlier times the *As* of money, like the As of weight, contained 5053.296 grains. The relative value of silver and copper 250 : 1.

[2] Denarius = $\frac{1}{72}$ Libra.

### B.   Coinage of 217 B.C.

| | | | Weight in Grains (Avoir.). | | Value. |
|---|---|---|---|---|---|
| | | As (copper)[1] | = 419.986 | = | $.0105 |
| 4 Asses | = | Sestertius (silver) | = 15.0395 | = | $.042 |
| 4 Sestertii | = | Denarius (silver)[2] | = 60.158 | = | $.168 |

### C.   Coinage of Augustus.

| | | | Weight in Grains (Avoir.). | | Value. |
|---|---|---|---|---|---|
| | | As (copper) | = 240.632[3] | = | $.01305 |
| 4 Asses | = | Sestertius[4] (alloy) | = 481.264 | = | $.0522 |
| 4 Sestertii | = | Denarius (silver) | = 60.112 | = | $.2088 |
| 25 Denarii | = | Aureus[5] (gold) | = 120.224 | = | $5.22 |

[1] Silver to copper, 112 : 1.

[2] Denarius = $\frac{1}{84}$ Libra.

[3] It is not absolutely certain that the As in weight equalled four Denarii.

[4] Often coined as a piece of four Asses, as we speak of our dime as a ten-cent piece.

[5] The Aureus, though nominally weighing $\frac{1}{42}$ Libra throughout imperial times, became more and more debased by alloy and in size, till in the time of Caracalla it was worth about $4.40.

The relative value of the same weight of the different metals in the time of Augustus was, according to Mommsen: —

Copper to gold,   1 : 666⅔.
Alloy to gold,   1 : 333⅓.
Silver to gold,   1 : 12½.
Copper to silver,   1 : 53¼.
Alloy to silver,   1 : 26⅔.
Copper to alloy,   1 : 2.

## TABLE VII.

MONTHS OF THE JULIAN CALENDAR WITH ENGLISH EQUIVALENTS.

| | Januarius. Sextilis. (Augustus.) December. | Februarius. | Martius. Maius. Iulius. October. | Aprilis. Iunius. September. November. |
|---|---|---|---|---|
| 1 | Kal. Ian. | Kal. Feb. | Kal. Mar. | Kal. Apr. |
| 2 | iv. Non. Ian. | iv. Non. Feb. | vi. Non. Mar. | iv. Non. Apr. |
| 3 | iii. " " | iii. " " | v. " " | iii. " " |
| 4 | Prid. " " | Prid. " " | iv. " " | Prid. " " |
| 5 | Non. Ian. | Non. Feb. | iii. " " | Non. Apr. |
| 6 | viii. Id. " | viii. Id. Feb. | Prid. " " | viii. Id. " |
| 7 | vii. " " | vii. " " | Non. Mar. | vii. " " |
| 8 | vi. " " | vi. " " | viii. Id. Mar. | vi. " " |
| 9 | v. " " | v. " " | vii. " " | v. " " |
| 10 | iv. " " | iv. " " | vi. " " | iv. " " |
| 11 | iii. " " | iii. " " | v. " " | iii. " " |
| 12 | Prid. " " | Prid. " " | iv. " " | Prid. " " |
| 13 | Id. Ian. | Id. Feb. | iii. " " | Id. Apr. |
| 14 | xix. Kal. Feb. | xvi. Kal. Mar. | Prid. " " | xviii. Kal. Mar. |
| 15 | xviii. " " | xv. " " | Id. Mar. | xvii. " " |
| 16 | xvii. " " | xiv. " " | xvii. Kal. Apr. | xvi. " " |
| 17 | xvi. " " | xiii. " " | xvi. " " | xv. " " |
| 18 | xv. " " | xii. " " | xv. " " | xiv. " " |
| 19 | xiv. " " | xi. " " | xiv. " " | xiii. " " |
| 20 | xiii. " " | x. " " | xiii. " " | xii. " " |
| 21 | xii. " " | ix. " " | xii. " " | xi. " " |
| 22 | xi. " " | viii. " " | xi. " " | x. " " |
| 23 | x. " " | vii. " " | x. " " | ix. " " |
| 24 | ix. " " | vi. " " | ix. " " | viii. " " |
| 25 | viii. " " | v. " " | viii. " " | vii. " " |
| 26 | vii. " " | iv. " " | vii. " " | vi. " " |
| 27 | vi. " " | iii. " " | vi. " " | v. " " |
| 28 | v. " " | Prid. " " | v. " " | iv. " " |
| 29 | iv. " " | | iv. " " | iii. " " |
| 30 | iii. " " | | iii. " " | Prid. " " |
| 31 | Prid. " " | | Prid. " " | |

To February was added, every fourth year, an extra day (*dies intercalaris*), which had its place after the vii. Kal. Mar., *i.e.* Feb. 23d.

## TABLE VIII.

### The Roman Day.

|  | | Summer Solstice. | Winter Solstice. |
|---|---|---|---|
| Sunrise . . . . . . | | 4.27    A. M. | 7.33    A. M. |
| 1st hour ends . . . . | | 5.42½    " | 8.17½    " |
| 2d    "      "    . . . . . | | 6.58    " | 9.2    " |
| 3d    "      "    . . . . . | | 8.13½    " | 9.46½    " |
| 4th    "      "    . . . . . | | 9.29    " | 10.31    " |
| 5th    "      "    . . . . . | | 10.44½    " | 11.15½    " |
| 6th    "      "    . . . . . | | 12.    M. | 12.    M. |
| 7th    "      "    . . . . . | | 1.15½  P. M. | 12.44½  P. M. |
| 8th    "      "    . . . . . | | 2.31    " | 1.29    " |
| 9th    "      "    . . . . . | | 3.46½    " | 2.13½    " |
| 10th    "      "    . . . . . | | 5.2    " | 2.58    " |
| 11th    "      "    . . . . . | | 6.17½    " | 3.42½    " |
| 12th    "      "    . . . . . | | 7.33    " | 4.27    " |

Length of day  hour at summer solstice,  75½ minutes.
"     "  night  "      "      "      "      44½    "
"     "  day    "    " winter      "      44½    "
"     "  night  "      "      "      "      75½    "

# INDEX.